*f*P

US

TRANSFORMING OURSELVES
AND THE RELATIONSHIPS
THAT MATTER MOST

Lisa Oz

Free Press

NEW YORK LONDON TORONTO SYDNEY

NOTE TO READERS

This publication contains the opinions and ideas of its author. It is intended to provide helpful and informative material on the subjects addressed in the publication. It is sold with the understanding that the author and publisher are not engaged in rendering medical, health, or any other kind of personal professional services in the book. The reader should consult his or her medical, health, or other competent professional before adopting any of the suggestions in this book or drawing inferences from it.

The author and publisher specifically disclaim all responsibility for any liability, loss, or risk, personal or otherwise, which is incurred as a consequence, directly or indirectly, of the use and application of any of the contents of this book.

Free Press
A Division of Simon & Schuster, Inc.
1230 Avenue of the Americas
New York, NY 10020

First Free Press hardcover edition April 2010

FREE PRESS and colophon are trademarks of Simon & Schuster, Inc.

For information about special discounts for bulk purchases, please contact Simon & Schuster Special Sales at 1-866-506-1949 or business@simonandschuster.com

The Simon & Schuster Speakers Bureau can bring authors to your live event. For more information or to book an event contact the Simon & Schuster Speakers Bureau at 1-866-248-3049 or visit our website at www.simonspeakers.com.

Designed by Paul Dippolito

Manufactured in the United States of America

1   3   5   7   9   10   8   6   4   2

Library of Congress Cataloging-in-Publication Data is available.

ISBN 978-1-4391-2392-8

We are one, after all, you and I. Together we suffer, together exist, and forever will re-create each other.

—PIERRE TEILHARD DE CHARDIN

Contents

Foreword

Mehmet Oz, MD

Few husbands are placed in danger's way by agreeing to write the foreword to their spouse's book. I insisted on this mission in part to gain earlier access to the manuscript, but also because my wife of a quarter century has been the driving force for so much good that our family has enjoyed. I wanted to understand what was going on in her mind as she developed a life philosophy that raised four great kids and tamed me.

Lisa has helped me watch the real action amid the cacophony of often mindless activity that we mistake for life. Like many of you, I have, at times, had trouble telling the difference between motion and progress. In fact, medicine has been a wonderful refuge for me because so many of the conversations we have are driven by a desire to treat illness, which makes them authentic. And even in medicine I have struggled to find the raw, honest emotion that touches our souls and have often failed utterly when trying to find these connections at home. Lisa's coaching, which she shares in *US*, has provided a crutch that many besides me can benefit from.

Lisa would have been a shaman in a past life. Many of her profound insights, gathered from spiritual and intellectual leaders who have blessed our lives, would have seeped into our life experience in bygone eras through ceremonies and rituals. Many are lost in the complexity of the modern world, where we can listen to whatever tunes we desire at any time but have trouble hearing the cries for help from those closest to us. As I read and reread *Us*, I remember late-night conversations that I only partly understood. Now I have the luxury of Lisa's well-mapped manuscript to remind me of the nuances that make the insights all the more magical. Although the book is accessible to the male mind, its message will profoundly resonate with women because the feminine mind is already seeking these answers. How do I know? Many of the strong women in my life (I have over twenty cousins and only one is male) feel instinctively that they need to live in relationship, but they have trouble explaining why they feel what they feel to their loved ones. Lisa's work outlines a path to explaining what you know in your heart, and her message has helped me immeasurably as I embarked on a path to teach health through the media.

In fact, the entire journey in books and television was Lisa's brainchild. Ten years ago, after hearing one too many stories of my frustration with the disease-focused care that I was trained to deliver, Lisa challenged me to write about my experiences. The resulting book, *Healing from the Heart*, was a catharsis and opened my eyes to the opportunity to teach in the public forum. Since she was an actress and producer, as well as mother to our four children, Lisa then created and executive-produced *Second Opinion*, a Discovery Channel TV show that brought thirteen hours of basic health education to the living rooms of families around the world. Ms. Oprah Winfrey agreed to participate as a guest on the inaugural show, and when her show kindly reciprocated, I matriculated at Oprah University, where she and her team educated me about the subtle aspects of sharing information with an audience. Lisa even predicted the eventual creation of *The Dr. Oz Show*, which arose from this experience, years before it even crossed my mind.

I also felt that the topic and title of this book was poetic justice. Lisa is a coauthor of all the *YOU* books that we have written with our wonderful collaborator Dr. Mike Roizen. She pushed Mike and me to create an edgy text that made often tedious medical material accessible to the average woman, who is ultimately charged with caring for the family. She also rejected the sour and dour emotional stories that often dot medical books and argued that although these capture the imagination of women, they don't help them communicate the health message to their fathers, husbands, and sons. The result is called nagging. Representative of this philosophy is the title of the book. Short and to the point, the *YOU* title emphasized that the book was completely about you, and that we weren't going to waste your time with nonessential material. The only topic we left out was the deep relationship talk that a couple of male docs might not have pulled off that well anyway. So Lisa compiled this information over the past five years as we crafted a series of successful *YOU* books, and aptly decided to call the incubated result *US*.

Lisa's decision to write a book also brings joy to my heart because I have always felt myself an inadequate student of her insights. Like many men, I have often found that my spouse's advice has come fast and furiously and just when I am jealously guarding my time while brainstorming about some project, now long forgotten, that seemed important at the time. The opportunity to harvest all her advice in one clean manuscript meant I finally had access to the crib notes.

So what is the essence of her advice? As a typical male, I quickly identified with her admission that it is really tough to change anyone else. I also loved her description of soul-mate love as both the destination and the journey. In fact, it is through erotic love that we approach the universal mystery as we consciously move from our feared aloneness into a merging with "the other." But Lisa's main message to me through all our years of marriage is that we need to live in relationship. She has always insisted on a "good" relationship that is approached consciously. And she highlights that relationships, especially those driven by conflict, push us outside our comfort zone, so I had to become comfortable becoming uncomfortable.

Lisa pulled together her advice through the years to create the work you are about to read. As a side note, I take this work very personally because I selfishly thought she wrote this for me and only got it published so I would have to read it.

She has organized my tutorial into three segments. She focuses on our connections first with ourselves and then with each other and finally with God. Throughout, she highlights that our faulty prejudices permeate our thoughts not only about ourselves but also about each other. In fact, emotions, like thoughts, have a way of materializing out of thin air. I have felt the brunt of them in a relatively serene environment when suddenly Lisa remembers something that I did wrong. Her irritation is usually justified, but we have both begun to realize in our hearts what we have heard so frequently from trusted mentors. To quote from the book, "Choosing happiness is not about living in denial. It's about living in and loving the present moment regardless of what that moment looks like. That's emotional freedom."

And like most families, we struggle with how to accomplish what we know we want to do in life. How do you distinguish between what you truly desire on a soul level and what your ego is craving at any given moment? Lisa frames the conflict by arguing that "what my true self wants is clear and specific, generally unwavering and long-term. When my ego-driven false self starts to whine, it's usually for something that just showed up." In fact, all the reasons we resist change condense into two motivations—seeking pleasure and avoiding pain. Lisa argues that "the key to real, lasting change lies somewhere between what you know and what you do. It's *what you think*. To shift your behavior, you need to start by transforming your thoughts. We all act the way we do because of certain core beliefs and the thinking patterns they generate. We do what we do because it allows us to live consistently with those beliefs—at least in our own minds. As long as those thoughts stay the same, our behavior isn't going anywhere—no matter how hard we struggle to change."

This topic is on my mind a lot these days. The more I offer advice to patients or audiences, the more I realize that the most profound and influential information is delivered in the ways described by Lisa. Her insights have always helped me personally, and recently I have realized that they crisply clarify the major challenge that I believe we face with health in America. You see, I think people today are better educated about their health than ever before in history but are not motivated to make meaningful changes in their lives. As a heart surgeon, I was trained to seek information when facing an intraoperative quandary. But throwing more facts at a populace confused about how to move forward has failed repeatedly. Lisa has convinced me that 80 percent of change is based on emotional insights. In fact, if a patient has a stroke that knocks out her emotional center, she can no longer make rational decisions. What a paradox!

And the most emotional connections of all are the relationships that define our lives. Lisa has spent much of my adult life trying to bring attention to these concepts, and I now finally have a masterpiece that explains to me (and hopefully to a lot of other folks) exactly what she has been talking about all these years.

Lisa has been my guide for our married life, helping me stay focused on the important goals we set together and avoiding the numerous pitfalls ranging from infidelities to perhaps the most treacherous demon of all, lying to oneself. She has a clear insight of what the "good life" feels like, and even though she struggles like all of us with reading the map instructions that take us there, her tenacious desire to keep our family on the bus as we travel in the right direction has made all the difference. All along she has emphasized a major message in *US*, that who we are is determined to a great degree by our relationships. We must find ourselves before changing the world, but paradoxically, we find ourselves best in relationship with others. And with the support of loved ones, we can overcome our impulses and connect the dots between where we are and where we want to be.

With the knowledge gained from Lisa, I have rethought much of how I motivate change. Remember that much of the activity that goes on when people are deliberating and reasoning happens in the frontal lobes. And when people try and stop a bad habit in its tracks, it's the frontal lobes that spring into action. Lucky for you, your brain has one really big frontal lobe, because you're going to need every last ounce of it to turn back the effects of a million years of evolution. Your mantra must be "Just say know." Not coincidentally, this is also where the mirror neurons live that enable us to see and feel the emotions in others and develop the most unique human sentiment of all, empathy. It is the ability to see the world as others do that makes us human and offers us the most tantalizing taste of what Lisa describes as living in relationship.

I have adapted my life to benefit from many of the insights Lisa offers and find myself more attached to Lisa than she likely realizes. Having spoken with many couples, I suspect that many women do not recognize how much their men desire them. Whenever you have attachments—to people or things or situations—there exists the inherent risk that they could be taken from you. This opens you up to the constant possibility of pain. Many men and women flee from this threat. I advise you to embrace the monsters threatening the harmony of your life and remember that God is not playing our game. We think this life is about winning or acquiring or achieving. For God it's only about connection. So your homework is to connect with someone you care for and tell them what you have learned from this work. I just did! Tag, you're it.

US

TRANSFORMING OURSELVES
AND THE RELATIONSHIPS
THAT MATTER MOST

Introduction: Who Am I?

This is not actually a book about "relationships." You won't find any tips on dating or rules for attracting the opposite sex here. This is instead a book about being *in relationship*. What's the difference? Well, the former is a thing and the latter is a state, and a state is part of what defines us at any given moment rather than something outside ourselves that we have or don't have. We all exist in relationship; we can't not. It's like magnetic force. Every object, by its very nature, exerts a pull on every other object. And whether we are aware of it or not, we are in relationship with all other things in this universe (and possibly other universes as well, but that's another book).

So, why is this relevant and who am I to expound on the significance of our place in the cosmos? Well, in answer to the first part of the question, understanding the nature of our interactions is important because the quality of our existence is determined by the quality of our relationships. What we believe, who we are, and who we can become are all manifest through our dealings with others. It is here that thoughts and emotions become actualized and our true self revealed. Our behavior is the only real measure of our character, and 90 percent of the time our behavior involves someone else.

1

And who am I? Trick question, right? Most of you probably know me as the wife of the "great and powerful (Dr.) Oz." But the wife of a wizard is not necessarily a witch—or a doctor. I am not one of those educated professionals who are qualified to tell you how you should be living your life. Rather, like you, I am a seeker. Sticking with the Oz paradigm for a moment, I am like the Tin Man, the Scarecrow, and the Lion all wrapped into one, striving for compassion and wisdom while I struggle to remain brave. You get to be Dorothy, joining me for a skip down a winding road. I will warn you up front: there will be flying monkeys, but I will try to keep the soporific flowers to a minimum.

At the end of this book we will have gotten to where we are going, which will be where we have always been. The difference is that we will know ourselves a little better. We will have caught a glimpse of *who* we are by becoming more aware of *how* we are in each of our relationships.

And I hope we will be friends. The title *US* in one sense refers to you, the reader, and me, the writer. We too exist in relationship. My intention is that you will see aspects of your own life reflected in my personal stories. My ramblings and musings are supposed to entertain but also lead to a place of connection. I have a hunch we are not that dissimilar, you and I.

So, now that we are going to be friends, I need to make a confession. This is an amazingly difficult book for me to write. See, there's this little secret among "self-help" writers that I feel compelled to reveal. Most of us are giving advice about the things we need to learn in our own lives. The wounded healer is one of those infuriating and delightful ironies of the universe. And while I never thought of myself as a "self-help" writer, you know where you found this book—right next to *Be Your Own Shrink* and *Why You Think Your Mother Doesn't Love You*—so you know what that makes it, and me.

INTRODUCTION

In the interest of full disclosure, let me state for the record that I am not the perfect wife, mother, child, or friend. Bearing that in mind, it is precisely because of the mistakes I've made and the lessons I'm learning that I feel I can share my insights. My wish is that they may prove helpful for you in your own journey.

This book is an attempt to offer the things I've come across that work for me (or at least that I'm working on). Please keep in mind that life is a process. I wouldn't for a minute pretend that I have it all figured out. I struggle in my relationships every day. So if you see me in the supermarket yelling at one of my kids, please give me a nudge and remind me to reread chapter 7. The important thing for me is to be *aware* and keep moving. The progress may be painfully slow at times. As Franciscan Father Richard Rohr says, "It's always three steps forward, two steps back." In reality, it's sometimes four steps back.

The ideas discussed in the following chapters are a compilation of what I have learned about being in relationship over the years as a daughter, wife, mother, actress, producer, and writer. In each area, I noticed that the lessons were frequently the same and that they would reveal themselves as long as I was willing to do three things—show up, do the work, and be honest with myself and others. It's a seemingly simple list—but not always easy to put into practice.

I have avoided, procrastinated, and fabricated enough for ten people, but I have also, on occasion, made a concerted attempt to commit myself to genuine presence. (Admittedly, even now this has not become a continuous state. Sadly, I am often looking at my BlackBerry instead of into my husband's eyes during a conversation.) But while I would hardly claim enlightenment, or even conversion, I believe I have grown. The concepts presented here are what I learned when I was *really doing* what I was doing.

Much of what I've ascertained is the direct result of the choices

I made, but I'm not suggesting that you run out and make those same choices for yourself. You can discover similar lessons and more exactly where you are right now. The fundamental ideas are everywhere, in every part of life—sometimes glaring at us like big neon signs, other times hidden beneath a surface of seeming insignificance. The truth of the matter is that we are learning about and living in relationship whether we're driving a cab or serving on the Supreme Court. The purpose of this book is to provide a mirror for your experiences through mine and to share insights that can be applied to your own personal journey of relationship.

One thing about life is that it often takes a *long time* to really get even the simplest truths. We can be sent the same message over and over and fail to see it. The problem is that we play out identical patterns with different people—repeat our mistakes because we live by rote—and then wonder what went wrong. To break this cycle, we often need input from a teacher, mentor, or friend who can shed light on our situation and show us what we need to do, where we can go deeper, and how we can change.

For me, those teachers took many forms. Some, like Father Richard Rohr and Reverend George Dole, came as real people; others were revealed through great books such as the Zohar and the Bhagavad Gita. After my parents, the most influential by far was and is Emanuel Swedenborg, an eighteenth-century scientist and theologian who saw the Bible as a divinely inspired metaphor, illustrating our spiritual journey. He described the path of regeneration, or rebirth, as consisting of a life of charity—which is essentially loving relationships. His writings on the nature of God, humanity, and marriage not only shaped my views on life but fundamentally shaped who I am. For this reason you will find his doctrine, widely and wildly interpreted, as the foundation for just about every chapter of this book.

Just to be really clear: none of the truly big ideas here originated with me. I merely applied the wisdom of my teachers to my own experience. In doing so, I came to the conclusion that all the important things in life are actually about existing in relationship. Of course there are other things, like brushing your teeth and fly-fishing, but my feeling is that ultimately these come back to relationship too.

So what, exactly, is the big secret about living in relationship? Simply what the great spiritual traditions have been teaching for millennia. Boiled down, it's essentially love God, love yourself, love everybody else. Why am I saying it again? Because I don't think we can ever hear it enough. I think we need to hear it, read it, feel it, teach it, taste it, speak it, smell it, breathe it, until one day . . . we finally start to live it. This book is my attempt to share the encounters and epiphanies that brought me back to that truth.

I've also included exercises at the end of each chapter. Reading about something is easy. Putting it into practice is another thing altogether—especially when the first time we try it is in the heat of a highly charged emotional situation. These tools are designed to help condition our reactions, so that we can respond in a more conscious way when we are engaged with others. I will admit right here that I am not a good tool person. I usually try them once, or at least think about trying them—okay, sometimes I just avoid them altogether because tools/exercises are usually work. These are not. They are supposed to be effortless and fun while creating a shift in perception. I want you to see what each chapter's key concept feels like when it's put into action. But please don't feel compelled to do them. Just use whatever you like.

The book explores the three areas in which we live in relationship. The first is our relationship with ourself. The chapters that focus on this topic are intended to help uncover who we are at our core and demonstrate ways we can integrate our inner being with the outer projection. Understanding our true identity is essential for any relationship, since without actually knowing our authentic self, we can never be genuinely intimate with another person. In these chapters, we'll also examine different ways of optimizing well-being so that we can bring our best self to all our relationships.

In the second section we look at relationships in a more traditional sense. We'll cover everything from our most intimate connections with lovers to the way we treat the homeless, paying special attention to patterns of interacting that maximize our mutual potential for personal growth. Topics covered include conscious parenting, sex as spiritual union, and compassionate living through environmental, global, and societal action. The exercises in this section seek to encourage generosity, compassion, and empathy.

At the end of the book we'll examine the idea of a relationship with God. (If you are uncomfortable with the concept of a personified deity, please feel free to use a term like "the universe." The divine has many names. Choose one that works for you.) In these chapters we're going to look at themes such as the interconnectedness of all beings as well as the function and form of prayer. The tools offered here include methods for cultivating gratitude, spiritual journaling, and a guided meditation.

These are our primary relationships. In my opinion they are interrelated and inseparable. We cannot love another person if we have no self-love, and the only way we can demonstrate our devotion to God is through our service for other people. *US* defines where we are in the broad scheme of existence and who we are at our core. So that's what this book is about: you, me, and God—US.

CHAPTER 1

You

This chapter is about *you*. Okay, I know, you're thinking this is supposed to be a book on relationships. And it is. And we'll get to that. But all of your relationships have one thing in common: you. You are the fundamental unit of every partnership, friendship, romantic entanglement, or antagonistic encounter you've ever had. And since you're the only part of your relationships that you actually have any control over, working with *you* is a pretty good place to start.

So, with that in mind, who are you? Most of us usually answer that question with a name and a list of vital statistics including occupation, marital status, education, and social security number. In our heads we might also include net worth, political affiliation, and preferred ice cream flavor—anything we feel attached to and therefore identify with. This includes habits, tastes, opinions, and emotions—those qualities that differentiate us from everyone else.

I hate to be the one to break it to you, but in case you haven't heard, that's not you. You are not who you think you are. You are none of those seemingly defining conditions or states. They're merely part of what Swedenborg calls the "proprium" or what Thomas Merton refers to as the "small self." In psychological terms, we've come to know it as the ego. It's a false persona that constructs a false reality within which to exist. Father Richard Rohr calls this false reality the "world of comparison, competition, and control."

Now, the ego's not a bad thing. It's necessary. We need to have something to work with—something to grow from. Our ego gives us each a unique playing field for life, where we can learn and create and evolve. The problem is that we think it's *all* we are. In reality we are far, far more. And less too. We all have a true inner self—a part of our being that can't be diminished or exalted by possessions or circumstances and has nothing to do with our likes and dislikes. It's not determined by our history or our attachment to material and emotional things. The true self is that part of us that's connected to all other life and yet is distinctly us. We don't often see it; it's frequently overshadowed by the big, noisy, dramatic false self. But sometimes we get glimpses of it through conscience, acts of altruism, and moments of joy. Mostly it is revealed in times of deep suffering.

Shifting your sense of identity from your exterior to your interior self is anything but easy. Generally it involves struggle, pain, and loss. The false self needs to die to let the inner self be born, and this death can be as traumatic as any physical death. But it's precisely the demise of what's on the surface that allows our essence to be revealed. This is the path that all the great religions speak of. In Buddhism it's described as letting go of attachment. Kabbalah uses the example of clearing the vessel so that the light can shine through. In Christianity, Jesus explains it in metaphor, saying, "Unless a kernel of wheat falls to the ground and dies, it remains only a single seed" (John 12:24). It's through this seeming death that our true life is able to emerge.

Understanding the need to go deeper into your genuine being is one thing, but how do you actually do it? Well, in one sense life does it for you. And in this respect, growth is far more an act of surrender than any conscious effort. When I was twenty-one, I was captain of the tennis team at one of the top liberal arts colleges in the country. I was zipping around town in my parents' Mercedes and engaged to the most amazing young man I had ever met. I thought I was hot stuff.

Six months later all my friends were in graduate school, and I was a fat, pregnant housewife living in debt in an apartment only slightly larger than my former closet. Not that my life wasn't wonderful. It absolutely was. But all the things that I thought made me who I was, the impressive As—attractiveness, affluence, athleticism, and academic accomplishment—were out the window. It was a bit of a shock adjusting to my new identity. But it also proved to be incredibly liberating. I gave up the constant effort to impress people because I no longer felt impressive. Losing the mask I had hidden behind for years allowed me to connect with others on a real level. The friends I made at that period in my life are still the closest ones I've got.

The irony is that if you live long enough, everything that you think makes you special, from your looks and your brains to your power and possessions, is stripped from you. You're left with what you came in with, and either you realize its infinite value or end up bitter over the loss of your fictitious identity.

But you don't have to wait until the end of your worldly life to start recognizing your true nature. There are many techniques for ego transcendence, like meditation, fasting, religious ritual, prayer, and certain types of yoga, which can help you separate from your ego-driven personality and bring you closer to identification with your true self. Regardless of the path you choose, you need to start with an honest evaluation of your current state. Only once you've made an accurate assessment of where you are can you determine what you need to do to effect change.

One of the tools I've found valuable in this potentially daunting undertaking is the Enneagram. An ancient system for categorizing different personality types, it is useful in helping map out key strengths and weaknesses, showing a way to use both for greater integration with the higher self. No one knows exactly where and when it originated, but it's believed to have been used by the ancient Desert Fathers in the fourth century and by Sufi mystics of the Near East for more than a thousand years. It was introduced to America by the spiritual teacher and mystic G. I. Gurdjieff during the early part of the twentieth century.

The purpose of the Enneagram is to help you see yourself more clearly—to reveal your distinct personality type. It's within this construct that you face your greatest challenges and opportunities for growth. Each group is defined by how they manage the basic fears and insecurities developed early in childhood. By seeing yourself through the lens of the Enneagram, you come to understand the different ways you meet fundamental needs and avoid emotional pain. You begin to notice that much of what you do is a reflexive response typical to your number, and not necessarily what you'd choose in a conscious, spiritually awakened state. Your evolution begins with this insight.

The descriptions here are merely an overview to give you a general idea of the nine basic categories. There is great variety within each group, as well as subtle degrees of difference, which aren't covered in this introductory summary. We're all unique, and none of us matches any one category exactly. You may not be able to determine your type right away. I couldn't. Sometimes you need to just sit with the Enneagram for a while before you see where you

YOU

fit. When you find your number, you'll know it. The self-recognition is astounding.

I remember having dinner with Father Richard Rohr, discussing the different types for about an hour, when my Sixness hit me like a tsunami. We had gone through each number several times and I hadn't found any that really felt like me. I have elements of all of them, as everyone does. Certainly I'm judgmental enough to be a One. I like to read and have zillions of books. Maybe that meant I was a Five. I knew I wasn't a Seven or an Eight, and I ruled out Six because among the qualities Richard had mentioned were fearfulness and a tendency to be a follower. You can ask anyone: I am not a follower. "No way I'm a Six," I assured him. He suggested that I could be a Nine since I was noncommittal. "But I *am* committal. I just committed to not being a Six." Richard smiled and continued with his questions. "What emotion describes you mostly?" I didn't know. "Is it anger? Happiness? Longing? Anxiety?" Oh, boy! When he said anxiety, it was all over. "What *exactly* do you mean by anxiety?" I asked, looking for a loophole—any way out of where this conversation was going. "Do you worry, have a certain apprehension about . . . well, everything?" he inquired. Bingo. That was me. I was worrying at that very moment—my thoughts racing between whether the cat had broken into the rabbit's cage and eaten him while we were out and what time the babysitter had to leave. "What number is that?" "Six," he answered matter-of-factly. "I'm a Six . . . Shit." I actually swore in front of a priest. He took another bite of his chicken and assured me that my response was quite appropriate.

The truth is I probably would have reacted the same way no matter what my number was. You might say I have a bit of resistance to being categorized as anything. If there were nine numbers, I was going to be a Twelve, dammit! Being stuffed into some labeling system felt limiting and pointless. Like most people, I want to see myself as ultimately indefinable.

11

But my real struggle with the Enneagram was based in fear: fear of the responsibility that comes with self-knowledge. Once you see who you are and recognize what you're doing, change becomes imperative. It's like looking at yourself in the mirror and, for the first time, acknowledging that you're carrying around an extra twenty pounds. It's never all bad (heck, my ankles are still thin), but there's definitely work to be done. Identification of your Enneagram type can be equally intimidating. Each number has specific gifts, distinct flaws, and a fairly arduous path that defines everyone in the category. When confronted by the self-revelation the Enneagram supplies, you'll generally experience both gratitude and dread. I must admit, the moment I realized I was a Six, my feelings were skewed a little toward dread.

I want to stress that the goal of recognizing your personality type isn't to fill you with self-loathing. Rather it's to help you isolate your specific areas of attachment and ego identification. As I said before, that is not you. You are the core of life essence that's underneath all the layers of false identity. The more fully you realize your own true being, the more deeply and unconditionally you can love both yourself and others.

Remember that no number is better than any other. Each one has its own set of advantages and limitations. Try to see where your type manifests in your individual talents and weaknesses. Often the same qualities result in both. Your greatest gift is frequently your downfall and vice versa.

The Enneagram Types

TYPE ONE Ones are idealists. They think everything (themselves included) should be perfect and are profoundly disappointed when they see this isn't the case. Actually, they get angry, but of course they don't show it, because, well, perfect people aren't angry. Since they have such great self-control, suppressing their hostile feelings isn't a problem for most Ones. That way they can go back to being perfect.

Ones want life to be fair, people to be honest, and the universe to behave in an orderly fashion. When this isn't the case, they'll set about trying to fix it themselves, or at least tell you how to fix it. They're good fixers. They will clean up crime, feed the homeless, and reform the tax code. Ones are also good teachers. They sincerely want to share their vision of "the right way" with others. Typically, Ones are the crusaders, the reformers, and the judges. They want to make everything all better.

Ones are moral, rational, highly principled, hardworking, and noble. I love Ones. For some reason I feel safe around them. You almost always know where you stand when you're with a One. They're so earnest and straightforward. If a One doesn't like you, it's usually because you've done something wrong.

The problem with Ones is that they can sometimes become self-righteous. Ones who believe their own dogma tend to be opinionated, critical, intolerant, and inflexible. And yes, we can all be all of those things, but when Ones are, they feel they're justified by everyone else's poor behavior. Ones can also be hypocritical. Once they realize that even they don't meet their own idealistic standards, they can give up on the attempt to *be* perfect and shift their efforts to the attempt to *look* perfect. The newspapers are littered with stories of politicians and prosecutors who have built their careers and public personae around stomping out some form of immorality only to later be caught seducing male interns or hiring prostitutes from another state.

Ones' ardent desire to be good isn't a bad thing. They just need to temper it with honesty and acceptance—honesty in addressing their underlying anger, and acceptance of the beauty in imperfection. They could also benefit from a little silliness, a good laugh, a naked dance in the moonlight . . . Okay, that might be asking a little much from a One. But by allowing themselves to let go every now and then, they learn to balance their sense of order and create a life of harmony and joy.

TYPE TWO Twos are the caregivers of the universe. They spend their lives looking after the rest of us so that we can go about doing whatever it is we do. They're the nurturers, the enablers, and the support staff: Mother Teresa, Florence Nightingale, and the biblical Martha all rolled into one. Twos' motto is "Sacrifice and serve." They love to be useful, to give you what you need, to be . . . indispensable. And there's the catch. Twos want you to want them. Actually, they need you to need them. Their sense of self-worth is almost completely determined by whether or not they're perceived as useful and necessary. Which of course means if you have a Two doing anything for you, you'd better fire off a thank-you note immediately.

I have quite a few Twos I'm very close to. Honestly, they are the most warmhearted, empathetic, helpful people I know. But I'm not a Two, so I'm not always sensitive to other people's needs, and sometimes—okay, maybe often—I forget to show my appreciation for all they do to make my life easier. Big mistake. When Twos feel undervalued, they can become bitter, manipulative, and resentful. Twos' favorite weapon is guilt. Lines like "I gave my life's blood for you and you can't even pick up the phone" are standard in the thwarted Two's arsenal.

Even when they're not in a reactionary mode, Twos can be a little suffocating; they are the original codependents. And while they're always ready to give, they almost always expect some form of reciprocation. They can actually be aggressively selfish in a deceptively passive way. If the motivation for their loving behavior is an underlying compulsion to get affirmation for themselves and doesn't take into account the genuine desires of the other person, then Twos aren't really acting from love.

In the same way that Ones can be too "good," Twos can be too "nice." Part of the problem is that they secretly take pride in their self-sacrificing. They know they're putting everyone else first and somehow that makes them superior. Twos could benefit from paying more attention to taking care of themselves. Getting a massage every now and then might help, or saying no once in a while when the boss suggests another working weekend. Twos need to be really clear with themselves about their hidden agenda and ask themselves what they're getting from their relationships. They can also practice giving with no strings attached. When there's no expectation, there's no opportunity for disappointment, and that way everyone gets a gift.

TYPE THREE Threes rule. And I don't mean that in some third-grade playground sort of way. They actually do rule the world. Look at all the high-level politicians, business tycoons, and media moguls, and you will find a shockingly disproportionate number of Threes. Threes are driven by the need to succeed. They are generally self-assured, social, confident, efficient, and ambitious. Today, in twenty-first-century America, it's a very good thing to be a Three. At least it looks like a good thing . . .

Threes are about appearances. They like to stay on the surface, where their accomplishments and charisma will win them accolades and hot dates. They prefer interacting with groups of people, where everyone can be suitably impressed. One on one and genuine intimacy is no fun. How do you win at intimacy? (Yes, winning is a big deal for Threes.) Whatever they do, they do it well. Not just well. They do it "the best!" Threes really get off on being the best.

Threes shine. Charm leaks from their pores. It's hard to resist a confident, energetic, attractive Three. They can't even resist themselves. Threes generally like being Threes. They think their success and popularity are all that count. They ignore the fact that they have a tendency to be vain, shallow, social-climbing narcissists. And they're often big fat phonies. Threes lie. Not the tall whopper that could get you to call them on it. They're masters of the subtle exaggeration, the tactful evasion, and deception by implication. The fact that the rest of us believe them isn't the problem; it's the fact that they buy the lie themselves. Complacent Threes live in a world of self-delusion. If Threes aren't really honest with themselves, they'll actually start to believe that they are the giant green floating head in *The Wizard of Oz* and not the scared little man behind the curtain.

For Threes to evolve, they need to be rigorously devoted to the truth. They also need to work in a little downtime, when they're not performing or achieving—a moment or two when they're off the stage and can reflect or meditate. (And no, plotting the next phase of global dominion and world conquest does not qualify as meditation.) When they learn to go inside with integrity, then their leadership can become truly inspirational.

TYPE FOUR Fours don't blend, they stand out. And they stand out with flair. They're the ones wearing the crushed velvet paisley jacket or the purple mohawk adorned with a single gardenia. Fours make an art of being different. They have a very defined sense of style and a unique approach to the aesthetic. Everything they do has a creative bent or a dramatic turn.

Their elevated form of expression isn't merely superficial. Fours are highly sensitive and emotionally self-aware. They're deeply introspective and intuitive. The realm of the unconscious, full of mysticism and symbol, has a particular draw for Fours. Death intrigues them.

It's hard for Fours to live fully in the present. There's always a pervasive sense of longing with them—a nostalgic desire for something that never quite was but should have been. Fours need beauty and significance, and they can see it in places the rest of us would never notice—in the symmetry of a row of trash bins or the irony and poignancy of a beggar on Fifth Avenue. Fours make great poets, actors, and painters. The rest of us can do it, but we don't have the art embedded in our souls.

Fours' need to be special often drives them away from relationships and genuine connection. They're so in touch with their own feelings that they can let those feelings become their only reality. This self-absorption can lead to isolation and alienation. They're by no means easy. With a tendency to be moody anyway, Fours frequently slip into melancholy or outright depression. Even happyish Fours take themselves really, really seriously. Somewhere hidden underneath the layers of eccentricity and romantic nuance, many Fours feel lacking or unworthy.

Fours' work lies in resisting the urge to withdraw into their inner world. They need to detach from their powerful emotional states and refocus their creative energies into something outside themselves. Transcendence for a Four occurs not through more self-awareness but through outward creative expression. It takes a great deal of discipline, but when Fours turn their attention from their specific experience to the broader scope of humanity, they can bring true beauty into their lives and the lives of others.

TYPE FIVE Fives live in their heads and would prefer if you didn't bother them there, thank you very much. For the most part, Fives are curious, open-minded, and intellectual. They're not *all* smart, but they all like to think about things—much more than they like to *do* anything. Fives feel most at home in the world of ideas and abstractions.

They love to watch. They observe what's going on around them, taking in every detail but often failing to engage themselves. A bit aloof, rather cool and reserved, Fives prefer to remain detached in most situations. Privacy is paramount. Fives don't like feeling encroached upon emotionally or physically. Even moderate proximity can be perceived as intrusive. They don't like too much attention on themselves and have a hard time expressing their feelings.

Understanding the way the world works—how the pieces fit together—is the way that a Five attempts to control his or her environment and thereby feel secure. For a Five, knowledge is more than power; it's survival. If a Five happens to be afraid of sharks, you can be sure he'll be an expert on everything from their migration patterns to their reproductive cycle. I know one Five who hates to fly so much that she learned (theoretically) how to land a plane in case both pilots had heart attacks.

Fives like to collect things as well as information. Cameras are usually a Five's favorite possession, but they gravitate to any technology-based gadget. They don't actually need much and pride themselves on their moderate lifestyles, but they aren't particularly generous with what they're not using. Fives aren't natural givers. Even on the mental level, they are much more focused on obtaining information than on turning what they've learned to useful action. Deep down they sense an existential emptiness, and their need to know or acquire is, in large part, an attempt to fill that void. Ironically, it's only through consciously giving to others, rather than taking for themselves, that Fives are ever truly satisfied.

For Fives to grow emotionally and spiritually, they need to get out of their heads and open their hearts. By going from contemplation to committed action, Fives can begin to learn from their own experience. With this type of knowing, they won't need all the facts and will be able to live in the beauty of embraced mystery.

TYPE SIX I'm a Six, and I can't say I am particularly thrilled by that fact. But that's pretty normal for a Six. We're conflicted—mostly about ourselves. Now, for all the rest of you who happen to be Sixes—and I'm assuming there are a lot of you, since Father Richard Rohr tells me it's the most common type in the Western world—being a Six can be wonderful. We can be deeply loyal, trustworthy, hardworking, and affectionate. We're endearing and dutiful, sensitive and vigilant. Sixes can also be extremely brave under pressure. Since they're dealing with their fears all the time, one more instance where they have to overcome some real or perceived threat isn't that big a deal.

Managing fear, anxiety, worry—whatever you want to call it—is what Sixes do most. For Sixes, it's almost as if the worrying holds the world in place. It gives them—I mean us—a level of assurance just to be aware of all the bad things that could happen. One way some Sixes cope is by becoming counterphobic. They avoid the underlying terror by keeping themselves on an adrenaline rush, taking crazy, foolhardy risks like starting fights and driving recklessly. Other Sixes become almost paralyzed by their fear, calculating every possible outcome before they'll make a move. Then they'll second-guess themselves and be riddled with self-doubt until the next thing to perseverate over comes along.

One reason I initially had difficulty identifying myself as a Six is that Sixes tend to be a mass of contradictions. They're strong and weak, generous and petty, bold and fearful, passive and aggressive. Now, I don't mean some Sixes are passive and some are aggressive. The same Six will frequently act one way and then five minutes later become its exact opposite. So labeling oneself is not a clear-cut endeavor.

For me, the upside of being predictably unpredictable is that Mehmet never knows who he's going to wake up next to. Is it the nice, loving Lisa or the mean, sulky one today? This generally tends to keep him entertained and ensures that he won't get bored. But for the Six (i.e., me) it's emotionally exhausting. The reason Sixes are so variable stems from a fundamental place of reactivity. We don't have a firm sense of our own inner strength, and we struggle with the vicissitudes of life.

Sixes crave security and certainty. What Sixes need is faith: faith in themselves, in others, and in the underlying benevolence of the Creator. And here's the crux of the matter: shit happens. The world can be a scary, hostile, vicious place. But it's never as bad as the Six imagines it to be. When Sixes quiet their horror fantasies and simply dwell in the present, trusting that they'll have and be enough in any situation, then they will manifest their true power, which is courage.

TYPE SEVEN "It's all good." That's the Seven's mantra. Cheerful, vivacious, and enthusiastic, Sevens sparkle. They seem to bring the sunshine with them regardless of the weather. They're full of genuine wonder and excitement. Snow White, with her whistling approach to what would seem like drudgery to the rest of us, is a perfect example of the Seven's mentality. That doesn't mean that Sevens walk around all day with a tune on their lips or a Pollyanna-ish grin on their face, but their natural inclination to see things in a positive light permeates all they do.

So what could possibly be wrong with that? If you were happy all the time, why would you want to change anything? Playful and fun-loving is a pretty good way to go through life. However (besides driving the rest of us nuts with their indefatigable optimism), there's a dark side to being so light.

With Sevens the drive for pleasure is motivated primarily by a deep-seated underlying need to avoid pain. They're unable to confront their own grief and fear, so they retreat to the surface, where they can keep themselves amused and distracted by activities or possessions. Beneath the big smile and happy-go-lucky attitude is a hollowness that Sevens would rather not face. By repressing anything negative and staying in perpetual motion, they try to skip along through the pretty parts of life.

The problem is that the void is still there and a few kittens and buttercups aren't going to make it go away. So what Sevens typically do is get more. The pitfall of a Seven is excess. If a pony makes me happy, why not just buy the herd. More, more, more, and the gnawing emptiness still isn't satisfied. That's when Sevens become hedonistic, debauched, and gluttonous. Life becomes a pleasure-seeking party, full of good times and high hopes but lacking in real connection or meaning.

If all the diversionary, escapist activities can't provide fulfillment, what's a Seven to do? As with each of us, in every Ennea-gram type, the most important thing is to be completely honest. Sevens need to acknowledge the unpleasant: the ugly and the painful in the world and inside themselves. They need to see their own suffering and the suffering of those around them. Sevens can also grow through practicing restraint. Resisting the urge to constantly acquire more allows them to fully appreciate what is. By allowing themselves to be present to reality, without evasion, exaggeration, or euphemism, Sevens bring a depth of sobriety to their happiness and experience real joy.

TYPE EIGHT Eights are all about power. Strong, self-confident, and resourceful, they embody the archetypal warrior. And yes, they love a good fight. They even love a bad fight if it gives them a chance to assert their might and prove their heroism. Eights are great defenders of the oppressed. While they shun the notion of weakness in themselves, they're ardent champions of anyone they perceive as helpless. They're fervently dedicated to justice and seek to eradicate exploitation and degradation when they see it. Undeterred by obstacles, Eights are the ones to call when you want to start a revolution.

Eights' self-confident and decisive nature makes them natural leaders. They're assertive, resourceful, and magnanimous. When they do something, they do it with passion, taking the initiative and taking charge. They're big-hearted and protective and will stand up for what they believe in. As long as they are in control, they will champion just about any cause.

But with very powerful people the potential for greatness is matched by the possibility of brutality. Eights' fear of being controlled can lead them to behave in highly destructive ways. They're frequently on the attack, seeing it as the best way to protect both themselves and others. When Eights feel threatened, they can become combative, vengeful, and ruthless.

Eights never back down from a confrontation. In fact they often seek it out and encourage it. Conflict is a way of connecting for Eights. They enjoy the struggle and seem to thrive on controversy. When Eights walk into a room and everything's quiet and harmonious, they'll deliberately stir things up. Eights' overt aggression and need for dominance can be intimidating to those around them and often prevent the Eight from engaging in truly intimate relationships.

For Eights to achieve real personal development, they need to let their guard down and allow their inner vulnerability to be touched by the world. When they add tenderness to their strength, they can become true heroes.

TYPE NINE Nines are lovely. They exude an inner grace and gentleness that makes them appear to be floating through life like wingless angels. Naturally easygoing and agreeable, they have a calming effect on those around them. Nines are optimistic and look for the best in people and situations. As the archetypal peacemakers, they have a calm, reassuring manner that makes them ideal at soothing discord or dissent. They crave harmony within themselves and in the world around them.

Nines are spiritually inclined, with a thoughtful disposition, and tend to overlook the mundane trivialities of human existence. On one level they seem to be living in a place that the rest of us aspire to, serene and accepting of whatever the universe has to offer. Yet their complacent approach can often become a way of tuning out everything that is uncomfortable or disquieting, and this is where Nines get into trouble. They'll do anything to maintain their peace of mind, even if it means disengaging from life. Rather than dealing with difficult situations or relationships, they retreat into a fantasy realm of euphemism and denial. Nines make conflict avoidance an art form.

Nines also prefer to avoid any kind of effort or struggle. Saying they're lazy might be a bit harsh, but they definitely have a degree of inertia—which is actually one of the ways Nines assert themselves. Good luck trying to get a Nine to do something they don't want to do. "Stubborn" doesn't begin to describe their level of resistance. They are positively immovable. This obstinacy is rare, however, since Nines' most common manifestation of lethargy is a passive "go with the flow" sort of attitude.

Identifying oneself as a Nine can sometimes be difficult. They share many qualities with the other eight types but often lack anything clearly distinctive. They don't always have a strong sense of themselves as individuals and often repress whatever needs they do have in order to accommodate those around them.

To claim their inner power, Nines need to become engaged. Rather than escaping into delusion and passivity, they must assert themselves and take decisive action. When they realize the true path to resolution is through the paradox of opposition, they can find true peace.

A Note of Caution

Initially you'll want to use this system to categorize others. That's not its purpose. The Enneagram is a tool for self-evaluation and evolution. When you're caught up in labeling those around you, you are avoiding the work you need to do on yourself. There's absolutely no point in musing about whether your boyfriend, who is behaving selfishly, is a Three or a Five. That's his job, not yours. Believe me, I know it's tempting. I constantly have to stop myself from using the Enneagram as a way of defining the people in my life. But the only purpose of understanding the Enneagram types of those you're in relationship with is to help you be more compassionate. By seeing that we're all just using different coping mechanisms to address the same uncertainties and anxieties, we can let go of some of our judgment and put our efforts into our own transformation.

Watching the Self

Now that you've read through all nine categories, see if any number reminds you of yourself. If so, try to be aware of how you habitually react as that type in your daily activities. Notice where your choices are influenced by the same emotions over and over again, and search out your subconscious motivations. Understanding them provides a more specific way of engaging in the journey of personal growth. However, if you use the Enneagram as simply another means of ego identification, a fun little way to label yourself—"I'm a blonde, a Leo, and a Four"—then it won't do you any good. And it could be dangerous if you were tempted to use it as an excuse for bad behavior: "I'm an Eight, it's my nature to be aggressive, so back off." The Enneagram can help bring your exterior self into alignment with your inner, true self, but only when the knowledge of your personality becomes a means to transcend it. You identify a pattern in your behavior so that you can simultaneously accept it and detach from it.

To do this, we move on to nonjudgmental self-observation. This is simply watching yourself without commentary or criticism— just noticing what you do and how you feel. By repeating this for a time, you'll start to sense two distinct identities. There's the you who's experiencing the situation and the you who's the detached observer. It may feel weird at first. But eventually you'll get used to your double identity.

The best way I can describe this is to compare it to driving in traffic. If someone swerves maniacally into your lane, you take it personally. The act itself is an affront to your dignity. You glare at them fiercely or swear as if they could hear you. Sometimes, if you're really offended, you may even gesticulate rudely. However, if that same crazy driver pulls madly into the lane next to you, cutting off someone else, you witness it without emotion—no outrage, no ego involvement—only the realization that the person over there is a dangerous driver.

By practicing nonjudgmental observation, you can come to view your own interactions with the same level of disengagement. Not so that you don't care about anything (I'm certainly not advocating for a society of passionless zombies), but so that you're no longer completely aligned with your ego. Because when you live in your ego, it's almost impossible to change. We are highly skilled at protecting ourselves. And if we equate our identity with our ego, we'll do everything in our power to preserve it—which usually means doing exactly what we've always done. Even when we know our behavior is making us (and others) miserable, we'll justify it, because it feels like a part of us. When all our energy is going into defending our actions, we're incapable of doing anything different.

But once there's even a hint of separation, and we can see that who we are is something other than the reactive emotional response, transformation can occur. This is where the real work begins.

Observation Deck

DAY 1. Pick a certain time to watch yourself—say, 2:45 in the afternoon. Notice where you are, what you're doing, and what you're feeling. Don't change anything. Just observe, without commentary—no labeling the behavior with "this is good or this is bad." Merely become aware of what you're experiencing without judging it. You might feel boredom or irritation, or perhaps a slight hunger or fatigue. Whatever it is, no matter what you're thinking, saying, or sensing, let it continue, but watch. If you start to do this regularly, after about a week you'll see a shift. You'll begin to realize that you are not your emotions. There is a part of you—your *real* self—that's separate from what you're feeling. When you stop identifying with your reactions and feelings, you'll stop needing to justify and defend them. This allows change to occur more easily.

DAY 2. Once you have the ability to see yourself outside of yourself, pick something in particular from which to create distance. For example, if you have an aversion to waiting in lines, choose this as the place to disengage. The next time you find yourself at a checkout counter behind half a dozen people with two carts each, watch how you react. Start with your thoughts. What's going on in your head that's making you feel annoyed or bored? Identify your thinking patterns about this event and then try to just let them go. Deliberately bring your attention to another thought—for example how silly the cover of the latest celebrity gossip magazine is—and watch your emotional state shift.

DAY 3. Use the nonjudgmental observation technique in your interaction with others. The next time someone does something that would typically set your teeth on edge, try to step back and witness the behavior without reacting. Allow yourself to let go of the need to interpret what the person is doing as good or bad, and just watch from a detached distance.

DAY 4. Try to determine your Enneagram number. First, narrow down the options. Rule out the ones that are definitely *not* you. Then, with the remaining two or three, see where each *could* be you. Remember we all have qualities of each number. The real question is what we are *mostly*.

DAY 5. After you've determined your number, list the ways you respond to discomfort, fear, or insecurity that are typical for your number. For example, if you're an Eight, you may become combative when you're threatened, while if you're a Two, you could react with passive aggression. Try to define your own particular pattern of behavior as clearly and specifically as possible.

DAY 6. Today you're going to turn an Enneagram-based weakness into a strength. Select a single behavior you want to improve. (Don't try to alter your whole personality at once.) Take this habitual action and reflect on it for a moment. Be grateful for the ways it has served you in the past and let go of the need to either defend or condemn it. Acknowledge that it is a choice for you, just as its opposite is, and at the next opportunity, choose to act in a way that is completely different from this typical response. Turn anger into compassion, deception into integrity, avoidance into action, and see how the old energy can be channeled in a new way.

DAY 7. Spend ten minutes in meditation on your true self. Start by visualizing the identity you project to the world—all your likes and dislikes, opinions and emotions. Then slowly, one by one, visualize them falling away. Those traits are things you have used to create your external identity, but they are no more a part of your inner being than that purple sweater you wore in fourth grade. Let each superficial layer dissolve until you are left with nothing but pure consciousness. Sit in that place and experience who you really are.

CHAPTER 2

Change

∞

Now that we've established who we are, or at least who we're not, I'd like to explore how we develop into who we want to be. One thing is certain: we can't stay the same. Change is the order of the universe. If you're not changing, you're dead—at least in the realm of biology. Though you may resist change actively or simply through inertia, it is inevitable. Ideally you don't just become something different (wrinkled rather than smooth, rich rather than poor, legally blind rather than nearsighted), you evolve; you grow, you transcend that "small self" in order to become a more mindful, insightful, loving human being. This, however, is *not* the order of the universe. Unless we consciously choose growth, we won't check out any better than we checked in.

Habitual Behavior

While genetics govern who you are at birth, what you *do* from that point on determines who you become. Sadly, much of what you do, hence who you are, is determined by habit. Which is not *necessarily* a bad thing. Habits help you function efficiently. Can you imagine all the energy it would take if you had to actively plan out your morning? "First, I will brush my teeth, then put on my clothes, eat breakfast . . ." When you were little, none of that came automatically. I still have to remind my nine-year-old to brush his teeth some days. And it's not just emotional energy, it's also physical. When you're performing complex tasks, your brain actually consumes more glucose. Once you do something repetitively on a regular basis, you develop a neurological system for storing that information that allows you to operate on autopilot.

We learn through repeated behavior. Our brains are designed to create neuronal pathways from one point to another, and the more often we do something, the more deeply ingrained that connection becomes. Eventually the response to certain stimuli becomes reflexive and instantaneous. This is very useful when serving in tennis, but not so helpful when trying to approach life consciously (though playing tennis and living with awareness aren't mutually exclusive).

My senior year, I went to a high school that was about forty minutes away from my house. It was a fairly complicated route, but by the time I graduated, I could have driven it with my eyes closed. Scarily, I think some mornings I actually may have. I had those roads programmed into my mental GPS (long before there was GPS), and for months after I graduated, if I wasn't thinking about where I was going, I would head to that school like a homing pigeon. I bet even now, though I haven't driven that way in over twenty-five years and couldn't give you directions if you asked me, if you to put me behind the wheel, I could take you there without thinking.

Habitual behavior becomes a problem when your whole life goes on this sort of autopilot: when you continually act and react without thought, merely because this was the way you did it in the past. Look at your daily routine and see where it has become repetitive and unconscious. I find myself in default mode just about everywhere. If I work out at the gym, I will always do the machines in the same order for the same number of reps. When I go to the mall, I hit the familiar shops again and again without even looking in others. And on Amazon I invariably search the self-help, religion, and decorating genres, sometimes cooking, but never ever biography. I'm sure it would behoove me to read something on the life of Charles Darwin or J. Edgar Hoover, but honestly, I never really think about it. It's just not what I do.

One of the things I noticed when I was writing this book was that my life was sounding a bit like a broken record. While wracking my brain for anecdotes and examples, I became painfully aware that the same themes were repeated day after day, year after year. Almost every story I recalled was about either overeating or complaining that Mehmet was not spending enough time at home. Frequently both. (Mercifully, I have omitted the majority of these tales, but you'll notice they still tend to dominate the pages. That's my life.) It was like I was caught in some kind of an idea warp. What I focused on was me being fat and my husband not being around, and what I seemed to be getting was more of the same.

And there's the crux of the issue. To a large extent you do what you've always done, so you get what you've always gotten. And this is fine when everything is exactly as you like it, but not so fine when you desire change. Which, by the way, is most of the time. If you need to lose a few pounds, your kids aren't doing well in school, you're not meeting your sales quota at work, or your husband would rather watch *Grey's Anatomy* than examine yours, then there is room for improvement.

Even when you recognize that you want to change, you probably go about trying to do it in the same ineffective ways that you've attempted in the past. How many times have you struggled to lose weight with a fad crash diet? Me? About three hundred. And that's just in the last year. Oh, and for the record, trying cabbage soup one time and lemon water the next doesn't count as doing something different. Same principle, same mentality—same result. With each failed attempt at change you become more resigned to the inevitability of a situation, then you give up and continue on the loop of repeat behavior. When we do something over and over, it not only becomes ingrained, it becomes boring. We become boring. We bore ourselves. Life loses its spontaneity and sparkle. There's nothing to look forward to because tomorrow will be more of what we did today.

Habitual Thinking

As horrific as it sounds, the most dangerous part of living unconsciously is not our boring, predictable, rote behavior. What we *do* is right up there on the surface for all the world (including ourselves) to see. If we can observe our actions, then there's at least a slight possibility that we can change. The real problem arises when our *thoughts* become automatic and repetitive. These are significantly more difficult to isolate because they're so deeply ingrained and have become so familiar.

Much of what you think is merely a routine response, having absolutely no bearing on your current situation. Acquired at some point in the past, it became a programmed reaction. Again, this is a useful tool for basic human survival on both the individual and collective levels. Ages ago a caveman ate a toadstool and died. Today pretty much everybody knows not to eat random fungi when wandering through the woods. At some point you probably burned yourself and no longer play with matches. This ability to learn from previous experience is highly beneficial. But if you take that same type of thinking and apply it too broadly, it becomes crippling. You fail one math test in third grade, so you go through school convinced that you're bad at math. Your boyfriend dumps you, so you approach every subsequent relationship with trepidation.

These conclusions are not necessarily true. You may be terrible at math, but you also may have just had an incompetent teacher. And even if you really are bad at math, just how bad are you? Can you balance a checkbook? *Bad* is a relative term. Unless you examine your beliefs, you will never know the truth and will go through life operating from assumptions that are most likely erroneous.

These faulty prejudices permeate our thoughts not only about ourselves but also about each other. How many times do we think someone is objectionable because they are different from us? We can be so sure of our own position that we condemn people for nothing more than an opposing opinion.

Yep, I do it too. I have certain instinctive responses that have become downright Pavlovian. If you mention that you are a personal injury lawyer, are a tobacco executive, or own the largest veal farm in Texas, I will instantly dislike you. Not that there is anything wrong with these jobs per se (except veal farming: it's barbaric).

Several years ago when my doorman mentioned that I had a new neighbor who was a litigator, all I could think was "I hope that ambulance chaser doesn't trip on my side of the hall."

The next week I was at the playground with my then-toddler son and was approached by another mother with a daughter about the same age. The kids were a bit hesitant about each other, but she and I got along fabulously. She was beautiful and really bright. (She had graduated from college at eighteen.) She and her husband rode motorcycles on the weekend, which I think is totally cool. And she was the eldest of six, as was I, but her father had died when she was very young, so she had worked to put all her siblings through college. I was smitten. She was my new best friend.

Hours later, with tired and hungry children, we packed up our strollers and headed into the building. We boarded the elevator together and I pressed the button for my floor. "Where are you going?" I offered, my finger still hovering over the number pad.

"You got it." She smiled.

"Oh?" I asked. "I thought I knew everybody."

"Just moved in," she explained.

I began rummaging around the diaper bag for my keys. My reflexive dislike response had just kicked in. She wasn't my BFF anymore. She was the new legal pariah. I wondered if she could sue me for not wanting to talk to her. The doors opened and we headed for our adjacent apartments. "I guess I'll see you back at the playground," she said, waving good-bye.

"Okay, see you tomorrow," I mumbled, trying to avoid eye contact.

"Hmm, not tomorrow. I have to be in court . . ." There it was—a full confession. I was done with her. "It's been a tough case," she continued. "Eight-year-old girl paralyzed by a drunk driver."

"That's horrible," I exclaimed, genuinely moved.

"Yeah, my practice can get a little rough. I only work with injured kids. It's hard, but I really feel like I'm making a difference."

Boy, did I feel like a schmuck. She wasn't looking for a quick buck from phony whiplash. This woman was a true advocate for the oppressed—oppressed, injured children, no less! I was so happy. I had my new friend back. And I had been forced to reevaluate an old prejudice.

That was a wake-up call. (I actually hate that phrase—it's vastly overused—but that's exactly what it was. Plus, I scanned the thesaurus looking for something better, and "alarm clock" and "buzzer" just didn't seem to fit.) At that moment I was awakened from what had been a state of unconscious reactivity. This is how most of us go through life until something or someone shakes us out of it. My behavior was based entirely on an unexamined habitual belief. I had been asleep.

I didn't stay awake for long. Fifteen minutes later I was back in my old routine, making presumptions based on a previous set of circumstances rather than experiencing the moment and responding consciously. But there had been a glimmer of recognition. I had seen the crack in my rock-solid assumptions. I was open to a change of thought.

Habitual Emotion

Once you start to observe yourself, you'll notice that your emotions as well as your thinking tend to be preprogrammed and automatic. Mine certainly are. You give me a scenario and I can tell you exactly how I will feel. Rude saleswoman at Whole Foods? Mildly annoyed. Script rejected by major studio? Utterly dejected. Droning dinner partner telling me for the five hundredth time how impressive her child is? Bored and contemplating feigning a heart attack to escape. How do I know? Because I've done it, over and over again.

On the surface all those sentiments are completely justified. Who wouldn't be irritated by insolence or depressed by professional failure? And the natural response to being seated next to bragging parents is invariably brain paralysis with a touch of desperate claustrophobia. The issue isn't really "Can I feel like this?" or even "Should I?" It's "*Must* I?" Do the events themselves determine my emotion, or can I choose how I will feel regardless of what's going on around me?

For the most part we are convinced that our happiness or unhappiness is the result of external circumstances. If everything is good, we'll walk around all day in a state of continual bliss. But if things get a bit rough, misery is our lot. This belief is based on the assumption that emotions are involuntary and inevitable. And they can be—if we go on living in a merely reactive way. But while most of what happens to us is outside our control, the one thing we actually determine is how we choose to respond to life's events. There is nothing inherent in any situation that necessitates a specific reaction from us.

I realize that it doesn't feel like a choice. Emotions, like thoughts, have a way of materializing out of thin air. We didn't ask to be angry or scared or depressed. But once a feeling shows up, we can either indulge it or let it go. The fact that you have a particular impulse doesn't mean it needs to stay with you. There's almost always another way you can interpret what you're going through. The whole "silver lining," "glass half full" approach to adversity is a cliché because people actually live that way. Choosing happiness is not about living in denial. It's about living in and loving the present moment regardless of what that moment looks like. That's emotional freedom.

Why Change Matters

So what's the big deal? Maybe your life isn't perfect, but it suits you okay. You're comfortable with your relationships and your opinions and you aren't particularly interested in reevaluating every thought or feeling that pops into your head. That's fine. If it's what you *really* want. If it's not a decision based on fear or inertia or habitual reflex.

The funny thing about choices made from those places is that they aren't really choices at all. There is no autonomy in reactivity.

Often what we do or don't do is exactly the opposite of what we say we want. For example, I would love to look hot in my tiny black bikini on the beach in Turkey this summer, and I know perfectly well that if I eat any more of my daughter's homemade chocolate chip cookies, it's not even a remote possibility. Yet the minute they come out of the oven, I'm all over them like a bear in springtime. Yes, I want to be thin, but I want the cookies too.

Okay, a nonfood example for all you skinny chicks who have absolutely no idea what I'm talking about. Say you're planning a trip to Paris in a few months. You decide you want to brush up on your French and figure you can spend a few hours a week in the evenings going over vocabulary. But somehow when you step off the plane, you haven't even managed to relearn the word for taxi. (Thankfully, it's *taxi* there too.) You simply had no time. Ah . . . but what about the hours and hours you had for *American Idol* or those reruns of *Friends* that you've already seen twenty-three times?

They were just there. And you were just there. And you just thought you'd keep the TV on while you glanced at that Berlitz book. You did want to learn French, but you also really wanted to know if the girl with the pink stripe in her hair was getting voted off. But now you don't even remember her name and you could really use the word for bathroom.

We pretty much always do what we want to, but sometimes what we want is in direct conflict with what we *want*. The problem lies in those opposing aspects of ourselves that I talked about in the last chapter. The needs of the different selves are mutually exclusive. When we give in to the demands of the ego, we are rarely in a state of positive change. Growth only occurs through the deliberate choices of the higher self.

How do you distinguish between what you truly desire on a soul level and what your ego is craving at any given moment? Well, for me they feel different. What my true self wants is clear and specific, generally unwavering and long-term. When my ego-driven false self starts to whine, it's usually for something that just showed up—in an M&M advertisement for example—and I need to have it right away. If I don't acquire it immediately, I get an angry sort of desperate feeling. There is no pressure from the true desire, but if you thwart the demands of the ego, watch out, you've got a death match.

Plus the appetite of the ego is insatiable. It wants the M&Ms *and* the late-night TV show, the pack of cigarettes, the bottle of gin, and anything else that strikes its fancy. You start with a few candy-coated chocolates and you end up passed out on the floor in a pile of ashes with an exercise infomercial droning in the background. Okay, I'm exaggerating, but there is some truth to this. (Although in this case I'm not speaking from personal experience. I don't even like gin.)

How you are in anything is how you are in everything. This is a concept I learned in one of my first acting classes a million years ago. I was studying with a brilliant teacher who made Darth Vader look warm and fuzzy. Deep down he was a pussycat, but on the surface he was more Komodo dragon. On about the third week of classes I arrived late, having circled the studio for half an hour in the pouring rain, trying to conjure up a modicum of parking karma. I finally skulked through the door and found a chair at the back of the room. I had barely sat down when Ivan the Terrible (I kid you not, that's his name; okay, not "the Terrible" part) stopped the scene he was working on and ordered me to the front of the room.

"You're late." Nothing like stating the obvious.

"I know, I'm sorry. There was no parking."

"That's irrelevant. Everyone else got here on time."

I think I must have rolled my eyes—just a little. I was that kind of student. Apparently whatever I did gave the impression that I didn't think being late to an acting lesson was a huge deal: the veins on the side of his neck started to bulge and he proclaimed, "How you are in anything is how you are in everything," and sent me back to my seat to consider these words.

I admit I didn't really get it at first. I thought he was idiotic. Was he saying that just because I was late to this class I would be late to every other appointment in my life? That was ridiculous. I was on time to at least half of my engagements. But after studying with him for what felt like several lifetimes, I finally realized that the key to this concept was "how." How did I approach acting class? Well, honestly, I was a bit disorganized, passionate but not committed, and unwilling to make huge sacrifices. Want to guess what my closet looked like? Think I was good about keeping in touch with my college friends?

And how do you think I dealt with personal growth or change? Right, in exactly the same way: I knew it was a good idea and wanted to do something about it but pretty much figured it would happen on its own without too much effort on my part. Ten years later I was more or less in the same place in terms of my own development. Any changes that had occurred were the result of external forces, such as having children, and not due to any conscious behavioral shifts of my own volition.

This is the weird and wonderful part: it works both ways. Once you start to make a change in one area, that change can be effortlessly applied to everything else. I know it doesn't seem to make sense. How could keeping your bedroom neat have anything to do with sticking to your diet? But it's like building muscle. When you lift a thirty-five-pound weight over and over again, you'll find it a lot easier to lift a chair. Your newly bulging muscles aren't good just for dumbbells. So when you actively change behavior in any part of your life, that same change muscle can be used for other things. I know personally that if I make healthy eating choices, my writing is much easier. When I allow myself to wallow through the pantry unchecked, I find I'm more likely to procrastinate, dawdle, or daydream when it comes time to work.

Why We Don't Change

There are lots of reasons we resist change, but really it boils down to two things. Pleasure and pain. Those two experiences in all their subtle permutations are the primary motivators for every one of our actions. We make our choices because we want to feel good or because we want to avoid feeling bad. Of course it makes sense that we would continue activities that we liked, but why would we repeat behaviors that made us unhappy? Because on some level we associate even more pain with change or perceive a benefit from staying the same.

For example, I noticed in past conversations that I tended to be spending way too much time complaining. My friends would call and ask me how I was and I'd launch into a litany of things that were overwhelming or frustrating or just plain bad. When I'd hang up the phone, I'd feel drained and annoyed, but that didn't stop me from having the same conversation with the next friend who called.

I finally had to be really honest with myself and examine why I kept doing something that was making me miserable. The first thing I realized was that there's a certain perverse pleasure in negativity. It creates an odd substitute for significance. But the real reason I was doing it was to avoid pain—the pain of having my friends resent me for what they supposed was a cushy life. On some level I felt that if I could show them that things weren't so perfect over in my yard either, I would stabilize our relationship. Once I acknowledged the fear of pain in the form of potential alienation from my friends, I was able to address the actual situation itself and stop the unnecessary complaining.

Pain, or at least discomfort, isn't all bad. It's an essential element of that inner system that lets us know we need to change. It tells us something's not what it should be—we are not what we should be. That interior sense can reveal itself in many ways: as depression or anger, boredom or anxiety. It's that feeling of emptiness that underlies the sleepwalking state of habitual living.

And what do you do when you get that feeling? Well, I can tell you what I do—anything at all to make it go away. It's uncomfortable as hell and I don't like it. So I distract myself with phone calls, Internet browsing, and my personal favorite—eating!

Addictive behavior is the way we numb ourselves to inner pain. It's the method we use to stay asleep; it's like a giant snooze button on the alarm clock of life, and we just keep hitting it over and over. At some point we need to wake up to the reality that facing the pain we are running away from is our only path to true joy.

How to Make Change

Most of us have an inkling not only of how we'd like to be better but of what we need to do to get there. Rarely is our failure to act the result of a lack of knowledge. I doubt there's anyone out there who believes that doughnuts and french fries are health-sustaining. Additionally, everybody would agree that having a positive attitude is a good idea if you're looking to get promoted. Yet somehow millions of us who claim we want to be disease-free and successful continue to gobble down junk food and walk around the office with scowls on our faces. We don't really need more information. We need to *do* what we already know. Real change can only come about by taking action.

I have a friend who has struggled with her weight for years, which is no surprise: when you get to be my age, most of us have at least a few pounds to lose. The other day she told me she was finally taking control of her health and was going to do something about it.

"Really, what is it?" I practically shouted into the phone, feigning enthusiasm for her new resolve, yet secretly thinking I could employ the same technique for myself. Maybe it was a South American magic herb that would melt fat as you slept. That would be ideal.

"I've made an appointment with my doctor to get a complete physical." Her voice was half an octave higher than normal, due to her mounting excitement.

"And?" I prompted, trying to maintain my swiftly diminishing interest.

"Well, then I'll know my blood pressure and cholesterol and sugar levels and inflammation markers." Apparently this would be thrilling data.

"And then what?" I clung to the fading hope that the doctor would next proffer the magic herb.

"And then I'll have a baseline to work from." Translation: "Duh."

"Oh . . . great," I responded. "That's really great." Of course what I felt like saying was "I can tell you right now, just by looking at you, that every single one of those numbers will be dangerously high."

I continued the conversation just long enough to learn that this specific information would then inspire her to eat better and exercise more. No secret knowledge. No miracle pill. Just the same stuff we'd been talking about for years and never quite managed to pull off.

Now, if there's an area in your life where you really have no idea what needs to be done, then by all means, go out and educate yourself. But once you've got a clue, stop pretending that the secret to your eternal happiness lies hidden in the pages of the newest diet or self-help book. It's not there. At least it wasn't in the last few hundred that I read. When seeking to understand more becomes an excuse you use to accomplish less, you aren't doing yourself any favors.

The key to real, lasting change lies somewhere between what you know and what you do. It's *what you think*. To shift your behavior, you need to start by transforming your thoughts. We all act the way we do because of certain core beliefs and the thinking patterns they generate. We do what we do because it allows us to live consistently with those beliefs—at least in our own minds. As long as those thoughts stay the same, our behavior isn't going anywhere—no matter how hard we struggle to change.

Simply denying the thoughts won't make them go away. The more you try to resist or avoid them, the more they pop up everywhere. Instead of pretending they don't exist, start by using the nonjudgmental observing technique from the previous chapter. Be a witness to your thoughts. Watch them float into your mind without attaching to them or fighting against them.

For example, I have this notion that I can't stick to a diet. (Last diet story for this chapter, I promise.) Throughout the day, thoughts like "I'm fat. I need to lose twenty pounds by Friday. I can't zipper these pants" (which is not merely a thought but a frank reality) drift into my brain and swirl around until some other thought comes along and nudges them out. When I quietly observe them, they begin to lose some of their power.

Once I become aware of these thoughts on a conscious level and am not merely living in reaction to them, the next step is to ask what they mean. What is the belief that is generating these thoughts? In my case it's the idea that fundamentally I'm not a very disciplined person. Typically I will attack a belief like this directly. When I wake up in the morning, I'll think something like "I'm not undisciplined. I will be disciplined today." Then over the course of the next twelve hours this is generally what happens: I decide I'm having nothing but wheatgrass and air for breakfast, then promptly scarf up the children's leftovers. Hmm . . . not disciplined. Next I focus my self-control skills on my work, but after fifteen minutes and two and a half sentences on the page, I promptly sneak over to web browsing. Finally, in a last-ditch attempt at a successful day, I determine to make a delicious yet nutritious dinner for the children, until I realize we're out of broccoli and I absolutely don't have the time or energy to grocery shop at five in the afternoon. Where is the number for that pizza delivery guy? And so it goes.

The belief is so strongly embedded in my psyche that when I attack it head on, I'm actually working against myself. A far more effective technique developed by Byron Katie in her book *Loving What Is* seeks to undermine those beliefs before trying to confront them. In her approach, she has the reader ask four basic questions: "Is it true?" "Can you absolutely know that it's true?" "How do you react when you believe that thought?" And "Who would you be without the thought?" The purpose of this exercise is to begin to shift your core assumptions about reality and yourself so that when you choose to take action, your behavior will no longer be in conflict with your beliefs.

Another question that I find useful to ask is "Where is this not true?" So with my perceived discipline problem, I would make a list of all the areas in my life where I have shown self-restraint or diligence. After a few minutes of honest soul-searching, I come up with a number of places where I am highly disciplined: I have not eaten meat in thirty years—not a slice of chicken or a bacon bit. I have never been unfaithful to my husband. (I know, I know, he's totally hot, but every other night on call gets old fast.) And finally, I have never spent more money than we had and have always paid our bills on time. Again, you're probably thinking, "Big deal, your husband's a doctor." But seven years on a resident's salary in a one-bedroom apartment with two kids, a cat, a rabbit, and six rats is hardly the lap of luxury—even without the cockroaches.

My conclusion? I am not thoroughly undisciplined after all. In some places I struggle and others I do not. My new belief is "I can be disciplined when I choose to be." Now the question is "What determines when I have self-control and when I don't?" I think the answer lies in my beliefs about myself and my place in the world. I feel very strongly about eating with a conscience, integrity in a relationship, and fiscal responsibility. These are moral issues for me. Potato chips? Not so much.

That doesn't mean I don't think healthful food's important. It's just not tied to a core value. Once I understand this, I know that I need to generate more leverage if I want to change. So I've learned to link the idea of healthy eating to things that really, really matter to me, like being a better mom by setting a good example for my kids, or staying sexy so Mehmet stays interested. These ideas raise the stakes. Creating a compelling reason to change enables me to alter my beliefs about my choices and facilitates the actual transformation.

Next, I stop associating pain with the desired action. To do this, I adjust my focus. I find something in the new behavior that I can enjoy so that needing to be disciplined is no longer a factor. When you love what you are doing, or even just like it a lot, you get into what Mihaly Csikszentmihalyi calls a "flow state"; you lose track of time, and the external circumstances surrounding what you are doing become unimportant. When I'm writing screenplays instead of self-help books, I get into that state almost right away. So if I need to work on a book chapter that's particularly difficult, I'll start by writing dialogue. This part is actually fun and allows me to segue into the more challenging areas without a great deal of resistance.

Sometimes you just can't find anything even the tiniest bit pleasurable in what you need to do. For me, running is like this. It's boring, it hurts my feet, and it has the remarkable ability to make time stand still. (I once ran a mile for almost thirty-seven years.) In this case you've got two options. Either pick something else that you do like, or override the pain by incorporating another element that you're absolutely crazy about into the activity. It should be something you just can't wait to do. Since most forms of exercise are equally anathema to me, I chose to make running palatable by letting myself watch TV only when I was on the treadmill. I've recorded every episode of my favorite show (24) and now I don't even notice I'm working out. Not quite sure what I'll do when the season's over . . .

If the thing you want to change is refraining from an old behavior rather than incorporating a new one, you'll want to use a slightly different technique. Say you have an undesired habit, like smoking or using foul language. Then the best thing to do is just stop. Okay, I know that sounds ridiculous. If you could "just stop" swearing, you wouldn't have called the power-tripping TSA agent a "stupid bitch." What I'm talking about here is not resisting the impulse. Instead, disrupt the routine. When you catch yourself in the middle of the unwanted action (cussing like a sailor), insert a completely incongruous word, thought, or action (for instance, say "lemon custard," think about naked windsurfing, or hop backward). It doesn't matter what you do, as long as you disturb the sequence of behavior. I find it helpful to do something a little wacky, something so far removed from the original thought or action that it sends your brain for a loop.

Tony Robbins does this sort of pattern breaking in his seminars. I watched him take a man named Bob, who was so depressed he said he was considering suicide, and turn him into a confident, hopeful, and excited participant in life. Tony did this by humorously interrupting every time Bob allowed himself to get into a negative rut.

Initially, Tony asked him about his situation. He let Bob talk about the demise of his marriage and describe what a failure he felt like. Then just as Bob started getting teary over the details of his divorce, Tony suddenly interjected with "She left you because you weren't man enough for her." Bob was obviously taken aback but didn't know how to respond. Tony quickly followed up by saying, "I can tell because your balls are up there on the shelf." Bob was now angrier at being insulted than depressed over his divorce and quipped, "Yeah, but they're some big balls." The whole room broke up laughing and even Bob smiled a little. After that Tony renamed him "Big Balls Bob" and his whole demeanor shifted.

By teasing Bob, Tony was preventing him from following the well-worn groove his brain had created by repeating his sad tale again and again to himself and anyone else who would listen. Once Bob was no longer entrenched in his particular repetitive thoughts, Tony helped him readjust his perspective and see his situation in an entirely different light.

The next time you find yourself falling into habitual behavior or emotion, see if there is a story behind it. When you start to hear this story in your head, break the pattern by mixing it up. One way is to change nouns. For example, if the story is "I would be happy if only Johnny would get back together with me," try "My dog, Fifi, would be happy if only Johnny would get back together with me." Or "I would be happy if only Abraham Lincoln would get back together with me." Or "I would be happy if only Johnny would get back together with Paris Hilton." The whole thing becomes rather absurd and the story loses some of its power over you.

Another technique for change is to realize that you don't need to wait until you "feel like it" to start. The part of you that's comfortable with the status quo, that needs the security of knowing tomorrow will be more of the same, will resist all attempts to psych yourself up for anything different. The key is to act even when you don't really want to. This seems counter to everything we've learned about changing behavior. What we're taught is that once we generate sufficient motivation, the new behavior will come without effort. But often I have found the opposite to be true. Sometimes you need to just do it. The purpose and the passion will come once you are engaged.

This is what happened when I became a vegetarian. Right around my fifteenth birthday my mother announced she would no longer be serving meat in our home and plopped a stack of books on the kitchen table. Among them was *Diet for a Small Planet* by Frances Moore Lappé, which is still one of my favorite books. I had gotten less than a third of the way through it when I thought, "Okay, I could try this vegetarian thing." And I did, although at the time I wasn't particularly zealous about the environmental impact of factory farming or the inhumanity of our slaughterhouses. I wasn't even that concerned about my health. (I was fifteen, remember. "Sick" was just an excuse to stay home from school.) All my motivation—the dedication to conscious eating, the concern for the planet and its inhabitants, the understanding of the ramifications of polluting my body with saturated fat, hormones, and antibiotics—came once I had actually been living the choice.

Make your own choice for growth and begin to implement it right away. Start with something tiny and manageable. Something so simple it seems almost too silly to even bother about. If you want to make exercise part of your life, try just stretching for five minutes when you first wake up. If you want to play guitar, learn a single chord each day. Once you've done it several times, your brain will adjust and it will feel normal. The habit-forming tendency that we discussed early on can actually work to your advantage here. As you achieve your small goals, you will gain a sense of accomplishment and the empowering realization that you can do what you set out to. Gradually increase the intensity and complexity of your goals as those change muscles build.

Finally, using nonjudgmental observation again, try to determine what fundamental need you were attempting to meet with the undesired action. Was it helping you feel secure or important or valued? Be both honest and kind as you search your soul for your heart's true desire. When you can satisfy that deep yearning directly—with love or connection or a sense of contribution and creativity—then you will no longer cling to any behavior.

EXERCISE

Breaking Routine

For one week you're going to try to broaden your view of who you are and what you are capable of.

DAY 1. Do anything differently. It doesn't matter what it is; simply find something you do on a regular basis and alter it slightly. For example, maybe you always go to the last stall in the ladies' room. So today use the first stall instead. Or let's say you always brush your teeth before you shower. Try showering first. The point is merely to be aware of where you behave habitually and mix it up.

DAY 2. Intensify the exercise and change something about how you identify yourself—on the outside. So, if you always wear your hair parted on the left, switch to the right, or be super daring and get bangs. Perhaps you're the type of person who wears sweats all day long (like me). If so, dress up for the car pool—makeup, jewelry, heels, the works. Or maybe you like to jog to eighties music. Instead, borrow your teenager's iPod and run with T.I. or 50 Cent.

DAY 3. Ramp it up further. Try something totally uncharacteristic—something *you* would never, ever, ever do, under any normal circumstance. There is something so freeing about being unpredictable. Find something that you think defines you and break it. If you are Jewish, attend Saturday morning service at a local mosque. If you are Christian, have a Friday night Shabbat dinner. One bit of advice when choosing something different: always strive to generate love, compassion, and awareness. Don't go from being an animal rights activist to hanging out at a slaughterhouse. The point of this exercise is to become more aware, more conscious, and more alive. Don't cheapen your experience or debase yourself. So pick something new that will expand your capabilities and deepen your understanding of the beauty in life.

DAY 4. Look for a habitual story you tell yourself that is limiting you or keeping you in a negative state. Maybe it's the tale of why you haven't been promoted or why you're always attracted to men with a wandering eye. Take that story and look for everywhere it's *not* true. (You actually were promoted four years ago, and the boy you dated when you were a sophomore in high school was utterly devoted.) Write yourself a new story that changes the way you feel about your situation. For example, if you haven't gotten that promotion, make the story about mastering your current position or about finally getting enough feedback to know it's time to switch jobs.

DAY 5. Write a list of things that you would like to change. It can be anything from losing ten pounds to remembering your friends' birthdays. Generate at least five items, then pick your top one and resolve to take action. Put it on a three-by-five index card and tape it to your bathroom mirror to remind you of your new commitment.

DAY 6. Make another list. This time write at least five things you can do to implement the change you selected the day before. These steps must be specific and doable. For example, "Exercise" is way too vague, and "Eat only celery for the next week" is never going to happen. Something like "Do sit-ups, leg lifts, and biceps curls for one half hour while watching *Jeopardy*" is something specific you can realistically accomplish.

DAY 7. Think of the reasons you have resisted change up till this point. What do you gain by staying right where you are? Be really honest with yourself. Are you avoiding the pain of failure or uncertainty? Do you enjoy knowing exactly what each day will bring and how you will respond? Once you are clear on the benefits of not changing, write down what it is costing you. Make the list as detailed and personal as you can by looking for the hidden costs in relationships and self-esteem, lost opportunity and long-term regret. Put the plus and minus sheets next to each other and compare. When the price of stagnation becomes greater than the effort to shift behavior, you will have the motivation you need.

CHAPTER 3

Suffering

∞

Recently I attended the memorial service of a great man. He was a decorated war hero, a devoted husband and father, a brilliant and compassionate lawyer in a class with Atticus Finch. Illustrious people from all over the country spoke volumes of praise for a life well lived. But the words that struck me most were ones he had written himself nearly seventy years earlier as a high school senior. Read by his children, the essay was entitled "Before I Die."

In eloquent language he articulated the things he would like to accomplish or experience before leaving this world. The first was to make a real contribution to society. The second was to have adventure in his life, and the third was to know one true love. These are all admirable if not uncommon aspirations. His last ambition was one I have never known anyone to articulate—particularly not a seventeen-year-old boy. He wrote, "Before I die I would like to feel deep sorrow." He clarified this by explaining that he wanted to live life fully, to savor every part of it, without censure—or as Tennyson put it, to "drink life to the lees." He wrote that only then, having quaffed the cup of life, could he unhesitatingly reach for its companion, the cup of death.

What courage! What wisdom! . . . What lunacy. Who in their right mind wants to suffer? Suffering sucks. And yet it's so much a part of all our lives that the Buddha claimed its inevitability as the first of his Four Noble Truths. There's no denying it: life is painful. And yet, more than anything else, how we deal with life's pain defines who we are.

According to William Somerset Maugham, "It is not true that suffering ennobles the character; happiness does that sometimes, but suffering, for the most part, makes men petty and vindictive." At times I have seen this in myself and in those around me. A man I know who grew up during the Depression has allowed his years of scarcity to impact all his interactions. Though he has made millions of dollars, he is still fearful of dying destitute. And since, on a subconscious level, he equates money with love, he's stingy and fearful—not only in his business dealings but with his affection as well.

But I don't agree with Maugham entirely. I do know people who have experienced such traumatic suffering, especially as children, that they have literally "broken" and are no longer mentally functional. This is tragic and I have no way of even beginning to make sense of the profound sorrow of this reality. However, I believe for the most part it is not the experience itself that shapes us, but our response to it. While we don't choose to undergo misfortune, we do decide how we react to those events. Suffering does not necessitate degeneration. Negative experiences can also trigger something positive within us. Crisis offers opportunity for change, and pain can be the catalyst for transformation, our greatest tool in the work of ego transcendence.

I have a dear friend who radiates gratitude and optimism. I have never seen her without a big smile and a ready hug for everyone she meets. If you ask her how she is, she will invariably reply that she is wonderful. This isn't an act. This is how she truly feels. While her life has been filled with struggle and heartache, she sees each day as a gift and an opportunity to contribute to those less fortunate.

Eleven years ago she gave birth to a gorgeous baby girl. The delivery was difficult and the child spent several minutes without oxygen to her brain. The result was severe mental retardation, cortical blindness, and frequent grand mal seizures. Now a preteen, this lovely young girl is incapable of feeding herself, sitting up without external support, or using a toilet. My friend has dedicated every minute of every day for the last decade to making sure that her daughter receives not only the physical care she needs but constant emotional support and love. I have never heard her complain or even suggest that life has been unfair. She considers her daughter her greatest blessing and is thankful for every day they have together.

Now, you may be thinking that she's just a positive person, and you'd be right. But she is a better person because of the way she chose to deal with the challenges and opportunities that having a disabled child presented. She has grown in patience and depth. She knows the value of family and appreciates the subtle layers of human connection. Small irritants like inclement weather or bad hair days don't faze her. She is kind to everyone from the bus driver to her coworkers because she knows deep down that life is too short and too precious to waste with pettiness. My friend has all these fine qualities and more not in spite of her hardships but in large part because of them.

There are countless people who have used their own pain for both personal growth and as the motivation and means of improving the plight of others. Nelson Mandela, Martin Luther King Jr., and Bill Wilson (the founder of Alcoholics Anonymous) did not become hardened or debased by their struggles but grew in both strength and wisdom. Because of the heightened compassion and personal resilience that they gained through their tribulations, they were able to improve the lives of millions.

Around the globe in countries afflicted by war, tyranny, or poverty, suffering is part of each day. Hunger, disease, violence, and the loss of loved ones are the norm for millions of people. While most of us will never have to face this sort of devastation, we all have our private pain. It's not essential that we experience something horrific to suffer deeply. We all feel sorrow and loss. The question is, What we will do because of it? How will our relationships be influenced? Who will we become?

What's the Point?

Einstein said, "I think the most important question facing humanity is, 'Is the universe a friendly place?' This is the first and most basic question all people must answer for themselves." As we look around the world at all the seemingly needless suffering—death and disease and torture and cruelty—it doesn't appear to be all that friendly. Sometimes it seems downright hostile.

I have a friend who's been raising her only granddaughter, a brave and beautiful six-year-old girl who was diagnosed with cancer a few months ago. Last week her body rejected the bone marrow transplant that was her only hope for survival, and she passed away. This makes no sense in a friendly world. What could possibly be the purpose of such a premature loss?

We witness this sort of bereavement from a distance and we try to rationalize it. We tell the anguished family we're sorry and secretly reassure ourselves that it can't happen to us. We are saddened, but somehow our sense of the order of the cosmos remains intact. Yet when we are faced with our own personal tragedies, the first thing we ask is "How could God let this occur?" When it's our loss or pain rather than someone else's, then suddenly even the existence of a benign Creator comes into question. For some reason we think that if there were a God, he couldn't let tragedy strike *us*. Which is ridiculous. What kind of faith remains solid while millions of children starve to death but goes out the window the day we are diagnosed with cancer?

Of course the only possible answer to the lament of "Why me?" is "Why not me?" If the universe or God allows terror and violence anywhere, then naturally they are possible everywhere. We are not exempt from the reality of pain. On an existential level, once it happens to anyone, it has happened to us all. I think we all sort of know this deep down, which is why we are fundamentally afraid. No, the universe is not friendly.

Let me clarify that by saying that I don't think Mother Teresa was friendly either. I have heard from several sources who spent significant time with her that she was, in fact, rather curmudgeonly. But "friendly" is not synonymous with "good." So while the universe definitely appears to be unfriendly, I still think it is good.

Okay, a brief aside here. In the interest of political correctness I could keep writing "the universe" when you know perfectly well that I mean God. (And I'm pretty sure Einstein did too.) But if the name really bothers you, please feel free to insert your preferred term for a higher power whenever you like.

Since we're on the topic of God, in the context of suffering, we're going to have to at least acknowledge the big question. How can God be all-loving and all-powerful, since the one negates the other as soon as the atrocities of this world are considered? Either God wants us to suffer or he can't do anything about it. My finite little brain can't quite wrap itself around this one. At least not when I judge things on appearances. But one of the really great things about God is that he, or she (as the infinite would by definition include and transcend any gender specific identity, please use pronoun of personal preference), isn't concerned with appearances.

God's not playing our game. We think this life is about winning or getting or achieving. For God it's only about connection. Swedenborg teaches that God's will is that we all be happy, but not the "Gee, I just won the lottery" kind of happy. The level of happiness that God intends is the inner peace and joy that comes from union with the Divine. This is only possible through overcoming the proprium, or false self, and by actively surrendering to Love. The choice cannot be imposed. We must act from freedom, and for us to do this, the possibility of choosing Love's opposite has to exist. The opposite of Love can be defined in many ways, as hate or fear or evil, but where any of these are, there is pain.

While God never wants us to suffer, he uses suffering as an opportunity to draw us closer to him. Suffering takes us to a place where we are stripped of the illusion of our own power, where we see the futility of our superficial attachments and misplaced priorities. When we experience anguish on the soul level, we enter what Richard Rohr calls "liminal space," a place on the threshold between different planes of existence. All lines become fuzzy; our definition of everything, including ourselves, opens up. It is here that real transformation is possible.

About a year ago I had the privilege of attending a retreat sponsored by O magazine for women truly in need of a spa weekend. Sixty of them were chosen from thousands who had written in describing their lives and why they deserved a break. Each of the selected women had experienced pain on a massive scale. Some had lost children, others husbands; several had been raped. A few of them had undergone a series of tragedies, including domestic violence, financial ruin, and personal illness combined.

Over the course of a few days they were able to share their stories and find comfort and guidance from a number of therapists and counselors who nurtured them along a healing path. It was a remarkable process of connection and compassion. Among the professionals leading the sessions was the author Martha Beck, who is one of the smartest *and* wisest women I have ever known. Her own traumatic journey has brought her to a place of deep understanding of the practice of transcending emotional, physical, and spiritual suffering.

She introduced herself to the ladies and then was silent for a moment, feeling the energy of the room. After a minute or two she asked, "Do any of you know how a caterpillar becomes a butterfly?"

Several hands went up and someone blurted out, "It makes a cocoon."

"Right," Martha continued, "it builds a cocoon. And what happens in there?" She looked around the circle of women.

A middle-aged redhead offered, "It grows wings?"

"Well, not quite." Martha smiled at her. "If you look carefully at a butterfly, you'll see it's nothing like a caterpillar. It morphs into an entirely different creature."

The women all thought about it and acknowledged that, yes, butterflies were definitely not just caterpillars with wings.

Martha went on to explain that in the cocoon, rather than sprouting new appendages, the caterpillar completely dissolves. "If you were to pull open the cocoon and peak inside, you would see nothing but a gelatinous sort of goop." A few of the women cringed. "In order for the caterpillar to transform, it has to completely obliterate everything that is even remotely caterpillarish."

A dozen heads nodded in understanding. The women knew the meaning of this metaphor. They had been there. Martha was talking about the death of the old self. Getting it out of the way to allow the new self to be born. This was what serious pain had done to them. They had been obliterated. They had been reduced to gelatinous goop. They were living in the cocoon of liminal space.

The promise of this story is that goopy caterpillars can become butterflies—creatures of extraordinary beauty and delicacy. We too are intended for a magnificent new identity. Within our darkest moments lies the possibility of infinite light.

Pain Management

Whenever you have attachments—to people or things or situations—there exists the inherent risk that they could be taken from you. This opens you up to the constant possibility of pain. When you lose something you care deeply about, you suffer.

The Buddhist solution to this unpleasant reality is to shun attachment. I have a really hard time with this one. Even the idea of attempting nonattachment makes me a little angry (red flag for those of you paying attention). You could say I'm "highly attached." I adore my kids and my husband. I am very fond of my home, and "impartial" does not exactly describe my relationship with chocolate. Pretending that Mehmet means no more to me than any other man is just plain nonsense. And sorry, but gummy bears will never be equal to a Snickers bar in my book.

Given the very definite hierarchy in my likes and dislikes, I resigned myself to the fact that I would never make a good Buddhist and figured I'd have to come up with another method of coping with loss. Then last year I had a gift of insight that changed my understanding of the nature of attachment. (Don't worry, it has nothing to do with giving up chocolate.)

Mehmet was in the last rounds of negotiating the terms for his television show. People had always joked that we would have to move to Chicago, but I never really took them seriously. Then out of the blue we were summoned to a meeting with the powers that be to discuss location, and Chicago was the number one choice. I felt like I had been shot.

I can't say that I behaved very well at that meeting. I was highly emotional and probably offended everyone in the room. When they suggested that I stay in New Jersey and Mehmet live five days a week in Chicago and two days at home, I lost it entirely. I left the room defeated and depressed.

I spent the next week in a zombie state, getting out of bed only to send the children off to school and grab myself a giant bag of chips. Occasionally I would snap out of it long enough to browse through Chicago real estate on the web, but that would just make it worse. Ice cream helped, a little.

Okay, I know I was being silly. Honestly, what's the big deal? Chicago is a perfectly nice city. Lots of people like cold, gray, and flat. I'm just not one of them. Plus I told you I was a master of attachment. I was attached to the proximity of my parents and siblings, my twenty-year friendships, and my back lawn with its lilacs, peonies, and flowering cherries. I was suddenly overly enamored with my kids' school, the New York skyline, fresh bagels, and thin-crust pizza.

I wallowed in self-pity, was cranky and mean to everyone, and gained about seventeen pounds in three days. Most of the time my friends and family tried to reassure me. "It won't be that bad." Lies. "The restaurants are great." Yeah, if you like steak! Can anyone say "slaughterhouse capital of the country"? "The shopping is phenomenal." Better than Manhattan? I don't think so.

And then one friend said, "This really stinks." I was just about to rattle off my standard "Even the Bears are bad" speech in my defense when I realized she was agreeing with me.

"You're going to have a tough time," she went on, "especially since Mehmet will be busy with his new show and you won't really know anyone." My eyes got a little teary but I wasn't actually sad. In a weird way I felt good. I wasn't being told to get over myself or make the most of it. My frustration was simply acknowledged.

I hung up the phone and sat at my desk reflecting on our conversation. "Yes, moving would be hard," I thought to myself. This was followed by a small, almost imperceptible realization, "and I will be fine." It wasn't that I had changed my mind. I didn't suddenly become convinced of all the great things Chicago had to offer. Nor was I merely resigning myself to the move because I had no choice.

What had happened in that split second was a melting of the attachment. I simply didn't care if we moved. I wasn't looking on the bright side or throwing in the towel. I still preferred where I lived, but I no longer had that desperate feeling that I would die if I had to let it go. I released my *need* to have what I wanted. I let go of my ego-driven demands, surrendering to the reality of what was. It was an amazingly liberating experience.

Equally amazing was the phone call Mehmet got the next day informing him that a studio had opened up in Manhattan and we could stay on the East Coast. When he told me, I was very happy, but at that point it didn't really matter. Deep down I was absolutely okay with whatever the location ended up being. Now this is going to sound a bit wacky, but I think on some level that clinging to my desire had built up so much negative energy that it was impossible for me to actually go on that way. I needed to release the hold my attachment had on me. I had to either move physically or move on emotionally.

We all have stuff that we feel we cannot possibly do without. But the fact is we came into this world with nothing and we're going out the exact same way. The only difference will be who we've become. Even the people in our lives are impermanent. On the purely physical level, everyone will leave us or we will leave them. The measure of a relationship is the depth of commitment and the quality of the connection, not the duration of it. We can't let our fear of loss become an excuse for not loving . . . or living.

Though real loss generates profound pain, most of us aren't living with this sort of emotional trauma on a daily basis. Nevertheless, we don't seem to be happy. We grumble and complain about everything from an obnoxious neighbor to overcooked fish. We sulk and scowl and frown and whine. This kind of negativity is not transformative. This is nothing but making yourself miserable.

We talked about this in the last chapter—that your attitude and outlook are within your control and that being unhappy is a choice. But I want to take this idea a little further. Look at the ways that you might be benefiting from holding on to your pain. Does your suffering give you a way to connect (as when you complain about your boss to a coworker)? Does it give you significance and meaning? Does it give you a sense of control? I know several people who use their disease as a way of manipulating people or situations: "Oh, I can't do that. You know I have a heart condition." Rather than taking charge of their health and using the disease as the impetus for making substantial changes in their lives, they turn it into an excuse—and a tool for getting what they want.

My mother has a friend who has remained in an abusive marriage for over forty years. Every time she calls, it's with a long list of complaints about how her lout of a husband has mistreated her yet again. Of course my mother is sympathetic, but at some point she's got to wonder, Why does her friend stick around? What could possibly be the reason she enables and supports a man who treats her so horribly? The answer may be that the friend needs the pain. It provides her with a certain amount of security—she knows that today will bring exactly what she got yesterday—and this is better than the complete unknown. It gives her purpose—fooling herself into believing that she can eventually make him change. And it gives her a sense of superiority.

Playing the victim allows you to assume the moral high ground. If someone has treated you poorly, then that person is bad and by comparison you are good. You haven't actually done anything to warrant that feeling of righteousness other than take on the identity of victim. But if you don't use your victimization as an incentive for your own growth rather than a means of controlling others, then it actually prevents your pain from transforming you.

In addition to the real wounds we experience, we often choose to suffer for absolutely no reason at all. Much of our emotional pain is imaginary or self-created. That doesn't mean it doesn't hurt. It just doesn't exist outside our heads. We come up with all sorts of scenarios and situations that have very little basis in reality but make us anxious or angry and cause us to waste hours in a realm of self-imposed anguish.

For example, you're on your way to work and there's heavy traffic. Instantly, you start thinking about how your boss is going to react when you walk in late. You suppose that she will be mad, so you piece together your excuse. As you go through the fantasy dialogue, you get more and more frustrated. She says you should have left earlier. You say your car wouldn't start. She says this is the third time you've been late this month, and so on and so forth, until you wrap up the conversation with "I quit."

By the time you actually get to work and storm into your boss's office, you are so wound up you barely notice that she's not there yet. When she does arrive, flustered herself from being caught in the same traffic, you're no longer considering leaving the job but are resentful and surly for the rest of the day.

I can't even begin to tell you how often I behave like this. I have a whole make-believe life that parallels actual events. If the kids are late or Mehmet neglects to call, I immediately envision some wretched scene involving ambulances or strippers, occasionally both. My normal response to this self-inflicted anxiety is first to indulge it: I'll run through the scenario once or twice in my mind, imagining the worst possible case. And then, when I can't stand it any longer, I will distract or suppress. Roughly translated that means Internet surfing or cheese, lots of cheese. But recently I tried something new.

We were spending the holidays in Maine with my parents, enjoying the snow and each other. Mehmet and the kids' favorite activity up there is extreme sledding—a wrestling match at breakneck speed, over hard-packed ice, down a half-mile stretch of steeply sloping hill where the last person on the sled has the privilege of leaping off it before he or she is hurled over a cliff into the rock-filled waters of Casco Bay. Great family fun!

They'd been doing this for hours and I'd hardly given it a second thought until I saw our car speed out the driveway. "Hmm. Where would Mehmet be going, and why wouldn't he have come in to say good-bye?" I left the kitchen, where my mother and I were preparing lunch, and went out back to the sledding grounds. There was no one to be seen, only an overturned toboggan and a few plastic disks propped against a tree. Up until this point I'd been trying to ignore where my mind was heading, but now I gave in and actively searched the snow for any traces of blood. Rather than taking its absence as a good sign, I was now convinced that my youngest child, Oliver, had snapped his spine. I rushed inside and called Mehmet's cell, then his BlackBerry. Both went straight to voice mail. Now I was distraught.

I paced from the front of the house to the back and wondered if I should call the local hospital to see if they had come in. It was too soon for that. They'd only left ten minutes ago. I tried Mehmet's phones again—okay, about five more times each—thinking I could force him to pick up if I kept calling. Then I noticed they were ringing upstairs. He hadn't even taken them with him. This was a really bad sign. On autopilot, I headed for the kitchen to get something to eat.

One of the most common ways we (yes, I do mean I, but I have a sneaking suspicion you do it too) deal with any sort of discomfort is addiction. It can be as subtle as the cell phone or as insidious as Internet porn, but everybody's got something. When we try to evade legitimate suffering, we fail to address our core issues and miss a crucial opportunity for self-revelation, and what we turn to as a means of protecting ourselves ends up hurting us even more. By using an addiction as a way of dulling or avoiding sensation, we may temporarily escape something painful, but we give up our power. We lose our ability to choose our response to an experience because we never really know what we feel.

So, back to me and my search for nerve-numbing snacks. On this particular occasion I was perfectly willing to trade the possibility of personal growth for a bite of an anxiety-soothing cookie, but my mother was in the kitchen and I knew she'd pick up on what I was doing. I didn't want to upset her; I was worrying enough for both of us. Bringing her into this when there was nothing either of us could do would be cruel and pointless, so food (my anesthesia of choice) was not an option. Neither was racing around in a panic, since she would definitely notice the uncharacteristic hyperactivity. So I found a secluded spot to wait. This was very uncomfortable at first. I had to acknowledge that I was terrified and powerless. But I forced myself to take slow, deep breaths, and as I continued to focus on my breathing, my whole body eventually relaxed. Until that point I hadn't even noticed how physically tense I was. More slow breaths. My mind started to quiet. I surrendered to the moment.

When Mehmet and Oliver finally walked through the door and announced that they had just gone exploring down by the water,

I was overcome with gratitude. If I had not been in that place of calm peace, this would not have been the case. In similar circumstances, my initial self-protective response has always been anger. "Why didn't they tell anyone where they were going? Why didn't Mehmet take his cell phone? Was it really necessary to spend five hours outside?"

Anger is one of the most common and least productive ways we deal with our pain. Because it is such a strong emotion, it can mask many of the other less comfortable things we may be feeling—like fear, vulnerability, and heartache. It's also a way for us to project that pain onto others. On some warped subconscious level we think that by passing it along, we're getting rid of it ourselves. When we send negativity back in the form of punishment to those we think have offended us, we feel we have somehow restored order to the universe. Which is just stupid. Emotional pain, in all its manifestations, doesn't diminish as it is spread from one person to another. Like love, it is increased by sharing it with others, so hurting someone else to make yourself feel better never works.

Growth through Pain

So how can we address our pain in a way that will enhance rather than diminish our humanity? Well, before I start giving advice, let me just say that if you are going through something difficult right now, I am so very, very sorry. If you have found a method of healing that works for you, please continue on that path and accept my deepest sympathy. If, on the other hand, you are struggling with your pain, allow me to share with you a few techniques that may help transform it into something powerful. Again, none of these ideas were originally mine. They are ancient practices from the great traditions—ones we may have forgotten or overlooked or never really paid attention to. But they are there to help us through our darkest times.

First, determine whether your suffering is real or self-generated. By that I don't mean only, did you create the situation, but is it something you allow to continue? If you are miserable, figure out if you can change what you are doing or at least your attitude toward it. When you resist making these shifts, you are contributing to your own unhappiness and have to take responsibility for that. Ask yourself what you gain by choosing to be in this state and see if it is worth the price of your inner joy.

When the circumstances are beyond your control—when you have been afflicted by forces of fate or another person's malevolence—then make sure you allow yourself to grieve. Give yourself the space to mourn. For some reason this is no longer acceptable in our culture. We're told to "Cheer up," "Keep a stiff upper lip," and "Take it like a man." But historically people knew how to communicate their sorrow. They tore their clothing and put ashes on their head, beat their chest, and wailed songs of lamentation.

Not that you need to express yourself in such biblically dramatic ways. But what we do instead is merely repress our feelings so that they fester in our subconscious. We dull or ignore the experience by turning to addictions, both soft and hard, to numb ourselves and avoid the discomfort of genuine emotion. When we suppress the pain, it has a far more devastating emotional impact because we never process it. If we don't deal with it in a positive way, it stays with us, poisoning all our relationships, rather than giving us a way of connecting.

Often we'll try to rationalize what has happened. The truth is that there are no words to explain it because no sense can be made of it. Through the portal of pain we have entered "soul space," which exists outside of words. Our role here is not to "fix" or deny our suffering, but to bear witness to it.

Once you have embraced your pain, let it go. Don't dwell on it or allow it to grow. Move forward by living in the moment. Worry over the future and regret for the past are forms of self-torture. Forgive anyone who is even partially responsible for your ordeal. This isn't for their sake. It's for yours. Clinging to resentment, anger, and blame perpetuates and prolongs the anguish of the original assault. Freeing yourself from negativity through forgiveness is the only way you will ever fully heal.

To hold the pain, to be present to the experience, and then release it requires great strength, but this is the only way to consciously integrate the lessons of suffering. Using the principles of alchemy, we see that our transformation requires both light and dark. We endure the fire of purification, bathe in the water of hard-learned truth, die as the ego is stripped away—one attachment at a time—and finally emerge, like the phoenix.

But the suffering alone won't do it. As we discussed earlier, some people let their pain make them harder, crueler, and more selfish. We must make a choice, and that choice is to surrender. We relinquish our ego attachments and place ourselves in the flow of divine providence, trusting that when our anguish brings us to our knees, it has brought us into the position of prayer. Here we can open more fully to God, and our experience of pain will be transmuted from a soul-toxic lead to the gold of compassion, gratitude, and wisdom. The transformation gives us the ability to love and serve others more completely and in doing so redeems our suffering.

Martha Beck told another story on that women's retreat that I think perfectly illustrates the painful process and powerful result of transformative soul suffering. She used the metaphor of the ancient art of crafting a samurai sword. The master swordsmith first selects the finest piece of steel. Next, he thrusts it into the fire until it is soft and pliable; then he pulls it out and beats it. Again he puts it back in the fire, draws it out, and pounds it. Over and over he repeats this procedure until he has created no ordinary weapon but the strongest and sharpest sword known to man. "You," whispered Martha to the room full of women, "are God's samurai swords."

We all are.

EXERCISE

Going Out, Going In

DAY 1. For this one day vow to do no harm. Seek to bring no sadness or anger to anyone, at least consciously. That means no snapping, yelling, scolding, scoffing, swearing, belittling, disparaging, or condemning. Respond only with kindness in every interaction. I know this one's difficult, but you can do it. If a whole day seems too hard, start with one hour, then two, and keep building. If you stumble and are inadvertently mean, just start over and attempt to do no harm for the *rest* of the day.

DAY 2. Actively bring joy. On this day seek to bring gladness to those around you. It can be as simple as offering a smile, a kind word, or a small gift. Pick anything that you think will create happiness for those you encounter, even momentarily.

DAY 3. Ease the pain. Identify someone you know who needs either physical or emotional comfort and do something about it. Make soup for your neighbor with the flu or visit your lonely aunt at the retirement home. The task today is to make another person feel better.

DAY 4. Reach out. Find an unrelated individual or group— people in need with whom you have no direct connection. Make this day about helping them. If you have money, write a check. If not, volunteer your time. The point is to do something that will lessen the suffering of those less fortunate than you.

DAY 5. Forgive another person. Think of someone who has harmed you—someone toward whom you feel anger, resentment, or dislike. Acknowledge the suffering they have caused you and then let it go by choosing to release the residual pain that you hold on to. Forgiving them will free you.

DAY 6. Forgive yourself. Take a quiet moment and get into a relaxed state. Go deep into a place where you harbor a sense of self-loathing or are secretly ashamed. Do not deny or indulge the feeling. Just allow it to exist. Then release it, by recognizing that it is not part of your essential self.

DAY 7. Forgive God. Be aware of any resentment you have for life's not turning out quite the way you wanted it to. Take each instance of disappointment or pain and offer it back to God as something that has shaped you. Allow yourself to be filled with a sense of gratitude for who you are in this precise moment.

CHAPTER 4

Your Body

∞

Y ou may be wondering why I would put a chapter on health in a book about relationships. On the surface they do seem a bit incongruous. But since *you* are inseparable from your body (at least for now), its well-being is extremely relevant. Those of you who are going all woo-woo on me, insisting that the body is merely a superficial, ephemeral shell, need to come to grips with the fact that it is through the material world that the spiritual expresses itself. Your body, mind, and spirit are inextricably connected—to the extent that it's nearly impossible to precisely delineate exactly where one ends and the other begins. Many of your emotions are determined by biological factors, and what you think or feel has a direct impact on your physical health.

It is both your obligation and your privilege to care for your body. Keeping it strong, fit, and agile is one of the most important things you can do for yourself and those you love, especially if you're a caregiver—which is pretty much just code for "woman." (Yes, I know there are men who are also caregivers, but for the most part the role seems to come with the second X chromosome.) We daughters, wives, and mothers are the ones who make sure that everybody else is fed, cleaned, and clothed. We see to it that medicines are taken, doctors' appointments kept, skinned knees kissed, and hurt feelings mended. We're so busy scurrying around fixing everyone else that sometimes we allow our own health to fall by the wayside. We just don't have time. Everything else comes first—from baseball games and dance recitals to making dinner, even if it's only microwaved leftovers. But when we neglect ourselves, we become exhausted and worn out and are actually less capable of effectively caring for those we love.

So the next time you think that taking an hour for yourself to exercise or get a massage is being selfish, think again. You need to be your best self so you can share that self with others. Your health impacts directly how you feel about yourself and indirectly how you feel about everyone else. If you have low energy or chronic pain or are suffering from some debilitating disease, then your ability to function on every level will be affected.

I know this from personal experience. You see, I have a rather icky condition. It's one of those things that you don't really want to admit to—sort of like recurring gas or athlete's foot. I've got waxy ears. Usually it's not much of an issue, but on rare occasions the wax will build up causing pressure, pain, and partial deafness. When that happens, take cover; PMS crankiness doesn't come close to describing my demeanor. First of all, I can't hear what people are telling me. There's just this intermittent buzzing noise that indicates when someone's talking. And second, I'm so consumed with my throbbing head that I don't really care what they have to say anyway.

Honestly, waxy ears aren't such a big deal; it's not like I'm wasting away from dengue fever or a flesh-eating bacteria. But something about being sick makes me incapable of contemplating anything other than my own miserable state. I become self-absorbed, impatient, and highly reactive. The last thing I'm thinking about is connecting with someone else in a meaningful way. In general, whenever you're in a less than optimal state, you have a hard time fully participating in a conscious relationship. That doesn't mean it can't be done. It just takes a lot more effort, and most of us really can't be bothered when we've got a migraine.

This becomes a significant problem when you live in a society where more than 60 percent of us are overweight or obese and a large number of us are afflicted with chronic diseases. Whether suffering from high blood pressure, diabetes, congestive heart failure, or arteriosclerosis, millions of Americans are physically and emotionally consumed by their illness and are therefore engaging with others in a way that is far from ideal.

And speaking of being overweight, this condition may not be as dramatic as an acute disease, but it too has considerable bearing on how you perceive yourself and those around you. I know that even being just ten or fifteen pounds heavier than I'd like can be detrimental to my relationships. When I'm feeling fat, I'm more likely to be mean, snappish, and insecure. I have less energy, am less patient with my kids, and try to avoid social situations altogether. Being preoccupied with my weight keeps me focused on myself and prevents me from really being available to those around me.

Given my passion for food, the odds are pretty good that I will never be X-ray thin. And that's okay. Being healthy, physically and emotionally, includes appreciating what you've got and refusing to indulge in any form of self-loathing. You, like me, may have some excess omentum, but we can't put off enjoying our relationships until that day in the fictional future when we will look like Kate Moss. The fantasy that you will be perfect once you lose those extra pounds actually gets in the way of doing something about your real situation.

Rather than despising or denying your current figure, learn to love it so you can leave it. Obsessing over something negative actually makes it more powerful in your psyche. Release your weight by accepting it with appreciation. When I have to go to some fancy event and my dress is fitting more like a girdle, I look into my fifties mirror. This is a game I play in which I imagine I'm living in the past along with other full-figured women, like Jane Russell and Marilyn Monroe. Putting myself in a category with these curvaceous beauties gives me extra confidence even when the scale has been chastising me all week. It's not that I want to stay plump forever. I just make the most of it when I must. So if you're feeling a little rounder and softer than you'd like, embrace your voluptuousness. Doing so will actually make you thinner, since you won't be eating to numb your depression over feeling fat.

One of the best ways to improve your health is to listen to your body, which is always sending you clues about its most basic needs. Pay attention to what it's telling you, especially when it comes to things like subtle food allergies or situations that create chronic stress. Don't ignore its signals by dulling them with caffeine, alcohol, or sleeping pills. If you don't feel 100 percent, there's a reason, and that reason often boils down to one of several very common causes.

What's in Your Mouth?

The first item on the list of possible explanations for why you're not as healthy as you could be—and by far the most important—is what you are putting into your body. You know the saying "You are what you eat"? It's literally true. Every one of your cells is replaced in about seven years, and your food is what those new cells are made from. So take a good look at what you've got on your plate. It's about to be a part of you. Are you really *that* attached to the chocolate cake? If you want your body to perform at a peak level, make sure you're giving it good quality material to work with.

Begin by taking inventory of what you routinely consume and ask yourself a few key questions. Do you eat whole foods full of vitamins and enzymes and phytonutrients that will nourish you and provide the energy to keep you going all day, or do you consume empty calories that wreck havoc on your blood sugar and your waistline? How do you feel after you eat? Do you feel strong, comfortable, invigorated, or do you feel bloated, stuffed, queasy, or nauseated? When you wake up in the morning, are you bright, alert, and ready to greet the day, or do you feel sluggish, exhausted, or congested?

Answer these questions honestly, and be aware of the ways in which your body is trying to communicate with you about your food choices. If it isn't totally happy, change what you're doing. How you go about it is completely up to you. There are a gazillion diet books out there. Some are better than others, but you need to find something that meets your specific needs.

My personal feeling is that it's best to avoid the very word *diet*. If you're anything like me, you will deliberately eat brownies within half an hour of starting any rigid weight-loss regimen. There's some sort of perverse rebel in my brain that hates to be told what to do—even if it's me telling me. Making a shift to choose nutritious food is not a diet! No, no, no! When you eat consciously, you can eat whatever you want. You just need to think about what you're *really* doing. Are you eating because you're physically hungry or are you looking for something else? When I'm wolfing down a box of cookies, it's never out of starvation. The hunger pangs that most of us are trying to squelch with our voracious appetites are emotional and spiritual in nature and can only be temporarily quieted with french fries. Feeding the belly is not feeding the soul. I notice with my own food addiction that the more I indulge, the more my ego craves and the less it feels satisfied. This annoying law of diminishing returns applies to both nachos and narcotics. When I'm emotionally agitated—it could be boredom, frustration, anger, you name it—I go straight into zombie mode. It's like I have a switch in my head that shuts off, and suddenly I'm being controlled by some other force—a force that wants to eat, *now*! Mehmet has explained that this feeling has a biochemical component, that it has something to do with serotonin and cortisol and ghrelin and several other compounds in my brain, but when I'm in that state, knowing what hormone is triggering it is completely useless. The only way that I've found to stop is to just stop.

I realize that sounds sort of lame, but it works—at least sometimes. Now, I'm never going to be ravishingly thin, but I'm getting to the point where I'm no longer embarrassed by my body, even naked. What I've been attempting for the last few months as I struggle with applying the principles in this book is what I call the "Sit, Stay!" Yes, I may have named it that because we recently got a new puppy, but the maniacally eating zombie has about a dog's IQ, so canine training techniques tend to be quite effective.

What I've been doing when I get the compulsive urge to gorge on anything and everything is this: As I open the pantry door and begin reaching for the hidden bag of last year's Halloween candy (don't even pretend you've never done it), I think "Stop what you're doing and sit down," and then I plop myself down on the nearest kitchen stool. I only comply with this somewhat bizarre command because I've made myself a deal. I've promised Zombie Lisa that if I stay there for a full minute, when I get up I can eat whatever it was I wanted guilt-free. But while I'm there I have to have a little conversation with myself. I guess by now you're noticing a pattern.

That inner voice and I are getting pretty chummy. Anyway, it's got a few questions for me before I can chow down.

Question number one: "What *exactly* do you want?"

Answer: "Stale M&Ms." I can't be vague here. Saying I want to browse through the cupboards until I find something tasty doesn't cut it.

Question number two: "How do you feel right now?" (Other than "hungry.")

Answer: Usually, "A little anxious, tired, frustrated." Sometimes, "Scared, bored, lonely." When I'm cruising for that food hit, the answer is never "Great, fantastic, couldn't be better!"

Question number three: "How will you feel right after you eat what you want?"

Answer: "Full, numb, quieted, relieved." (Response varies but is generally of this nature.)

Fourth question: "How will you feel ten minutes after you're done?"

Answer: "Ashamed, despondent, defeated, and hopeless."

Last question: "Is this what you want?"

If I reply in the affirmative, I can go get whatever I was jonesing for. But usually by this point the tractor beam has been broken and I have my real brain back again.

The purpose of the exercise is to bring awareness to your eating, so you can get out of that unconscious, habitual mode that we discussed earlier. When you're awake and aware, you can eat whatever you feel like and it will probably be the right choice—even without sticking to a diet. It doesn't take a registered dietitian to recognize that hot dogs are bad and spinach is good. The only guideline you really need for food is this: if it was made by God, great. If it was made by man—which means processed, colored, homogenized, enriched, refined, preserved, and packaged—avoid as much as possible. If it comes from an animal, sparingly, if you must.

The food you choose should have a high nutrient-to-calorie ratio. Ideally you'd have lots of fruits and vegetables, legumes, and whole grains. You'd stay away from white breads, chips, cakes, and candies, and meat and dairy would be feast foods, not a daily staple. This is pretty close to the Mediterranean diet, which has been shown over and over again to be one of the most healthful ways of eating.

But remember that while being healthy is definitely part of the higher self's agenda, so is joy. So if eating spinach makes you gag, don't do it. Living consciously isn't about becoming a puritan. You don't need to give up the sensual pleasure of eating just because you select nutritious food. Actually, being totally present while you eat, savoring every bite so that you completely experience its full flavor is a key element of eating with awareness.

Detox

Once you've mastered putting good things *in* your body, the next step is to get the bad stuff *out*. The modern world is full environmental hazards. With all the pesticides and herbicides, agricultural antibiotics and hormones, flame-retardant treatments, petrochemicals, heavy metals, and radiation, it's a wonder we don't all have horns sprouting out of our heads and a fourteen-year lifespan. Thankfully we have built in methods of dealing with these external assailants.

Your body is constantly ridding itself of all kinds of toxins through its various systems of elimination. Helping it clear these more effectively is critical for vibrant health. Peeing and pooping are of course the most obvious ways we eliminate waste material. (And you thought Mehmet was the only one who indulged in scatological dialogue.) I know you've heard it a million times, but you need to drink plenty of water to keep these moving smoothly. Both the kidneys and the bowel rely on adequate water intake for optimal excretion. (If you suffer from chronic constipation even though you are drinking lots of water and eating enough fiber, try taking some extra magnesium with your vitamins in the morning. I've suggested this to innumerable friends who've had trouble with regularity and it's worked every time.)

Fasting is another way you can aid your body in getting rid of toxins. The idea behind restricting food intake is that when you reduce the amount of food coming in, the body can more efficiently work on moving out waste. A fast doesn't have to be forty days on water. You can do a juice fast or even eat a plant-based raw diet, which has a purifying effect. I personally like to do a modified cleanse once a year, consisting of a week on just fruits and vegetables, followed by a three-day total fast with nothing but lemon water and herbal teas.

Okay, that's not entirely true. I don't *like* fasting. I *like* to eat. Fasting for me is hard. I get headaches. I get bitchy. I get tired. And that's just in the first hour. Three out of four times I've started a fast, I've broken it within a day. But I feel so amazingly good when I actually complete it that I keep trying again. One thing that helps is to schedule your fast while your kitchen is under construction so that any temptation to cheat is thwarted by the mere absence of food. If major renovations are not an option, I suggest taking a weekend at a spa where everyone else is fasting too (especially if you've never done it before). But if you're going to white-knuckle it alone, here are some tips:

1. Start small. Try all raw foods one day a month. When you've done that a couple of times, move on to a simple juice fast. Stay away from the sweet fruit juices, since they will give you sugar highs and crashes. Invest in a good juicer and make your own delicious combinations of fruit and vegetables. My favorite is spinach, cucumber, green apple, celery, parsley, and lime. You can throw in a

tiny piece of ginger too if you like it. As the single-day fast becomes easier, you can progress to three days a month and work your way up to a week a few times a year.

2. Make the cleanse comprehensive. See if you can use this period to cut out the emotional junk as well as the physical. Avoid surfing the Internet and watching TV. Don't spend time with people who drain you, and find quiet time for reflection each day. Fasting brings up a lot of issues—especially when you are one of those people who use food to suppress them.

3. Enlist the people around you as your support team. Let your family and friends know what you are embarking upon so that they don't inadvertently sabotage your efforts by inviting you to a wine tasting on day four. My kids love making juices for me when I'm fasting, and they're really good about eating in another room so that I don't covet their snacks.

Another really important and much-overlooked element in the process of detoxification is sweating. Your skin is actually your largest organ of elimination and can excrete several liters of fluid per hour in extreme heat. When it leaves your body, that fluid carries all kinds of potentially harmful chemicals with it. Of course, the best way to work up a sweat is vigorous exercise, which also makes you breathe deeply—another great detoxifier. Alternatively, I love to heat up in a sauna or steam bath whenever possible. At least once a week do something that gets you good and wet.

The last area of cleansing I want to discuss doesn't really fall within the normal range of elimination but can profoundly impact your health. It's a topic that people don't want to discuss, let alone entertain the thought that they might have it, or in this case *them*— the dreaded parasites! Don't think that because you live in America and wash your hands every five minutes you're exempt. If you travel to foreign counties, eat sushi or unwashed imported fruits and vegetables, walk barefoot outside, or own a pet, the odds are you've got some. Symptoms include everything from fatigue to poor digestion, gas, bloating, muscle and joint pain, headaches, and food allergies.

Most MDs don't really consider parasites when making a diagnosis, and even fewer ever check for them, but the doctors' offices that do estimate that the vast majority of their patients have some kind of infestation. I had chronic back pain, though only at night, for nine years. I went to orthopedic surgeons and neurologists, chiropractors, energy healers, and osteopaths. I had CAT scans, MRIs, X-rays, and acupuncture.

After years and years of searching for an answer I came to accept the fact that I was destined to wake up in pain at about 3:30 every morning. By sheer chance I took a routine blood test that measured my C-reactive protein. This is a marker for inflammation in the body. Mine was seventeen! Good is zero. I seemed to be fighting some full-blown infection but there was nothing wrong with me—other than the back pain. Now, inflammation itself is not a bad thing. When you have a cut or a bacterial infection, inflammation is the body's response to protect you. But chronic inflammation can cause everything from heart disease and cancer to premature aging (yikes!). Lack of sleep I could live with. Extra wrinkles, forget about it! I tried treating the inflammation directly, but it held fast at sixteen.

I mentioned my situation to a friend and he suggested I go to a naturopath who had treated him for MS when he was in his thirties. By the way, this friend went from a wheelchair to playing football with his son, so I was impressed by whatever his doctor was doing. What he did to me was take my pulse, look at my tongue, and tell me I had amoebic parasites. These, he said, were causing intestinal inflammation that was radiating to my back. I was disgusted but grateful he hadn't said that anything that started with *hook, round, tape,* or *pin.* I'm totally grossed out by the mere thought of worms. Revolting little protozoan creatures weren't much better, but they wouldn't be crawling out of unsuspecting orifices anytime soon. Anyway, I took his herbs and within a month my back pain was gone and my C-reactive protein was at eight. Three months later it was below one and those evil creatures in my gut were gone.

Yogalicious

This isn't going to come as a surprise to any of you—especially not those of you who have followed Mehmet's work—but the second important factor in keeping your body healthy is keeping it moving. You can walk, run, swim, bike, or dance. Frankly, it doesn't make any difference what you do as long as you really enjoy it. If it's absolute torture every time you go to the gym, your routine's going to last about two visits. You'll throw away your locker key and be back on your reclining lounge chair watching QVC faster than they can sell out of Diamonique earrings.

My favorite form of exercise is yoga. It strengthens and stretches the body while it helps to focus the mind. I love how I feel while I'm doing it, and I simply adore how I feel afterward. I'd be hard-pressed to think of another workout that makes me so happy. Yeah, I know, yoga has a little bit of a weird reputation, but before you get all nervous, let me assure you that I don't wear Birkenstocks or eat granola. I can't bend myself like Gumby and I don't weigh less than my height in inches. I do like Hare Krishna songs, but I refuse to wear orange. And none of that makes any difference, because one of the really great things about yoga is that you don't have to be a yogi to do it. You can be short or tall, young or old, a super athlete or a recovering couch potato. You can take it slow and easy, or if you're one of those sweat fiends, you can crank up the heat and get the most vigorous workout of your life. Yoga works for everybody and there's no such thing as striking a perfect pose. You go as far as you can in each position, or asana, and that's exactly the place that will give you what you need. As you get more flexible, you'll be able to go deeper, but it's still about getting to a point where you are comfortable being uncomfortable—where you can achieve equanimity in body and mind.

The other aspect of yoga that is essential for good health (and is frequently overlooked in other forms of exercise) is its emphasis on the breath. We all breathe all the time, so we think we're experts, but taking deliberately slow, rhythmic, diaphragmatic breaths has tremendous benefits. According to both ancient yogic tradition and modern science, deep breathing can be effective in reducing stress. It's also an essential tool in detoxification, eliminating carbon dioxide and stimulating lymphatic drainage, thereby clearing the body of metabolic waste products stored in our tissue.

It's very possible that yoga isn't your activity of choice, and that's fine. But you've really got to try it at least once. You can take an introductory class at a studio or rent an instructional DVD so nobody will ever see you in "down dog." Just do what you can and remember that wherever you are is exactly where you're supposed to be. That's yoga.

Bedtime

My third recommendation for staying healthy—no smirking here—is getting enough sleep. How do you know what's enough? Well, here's a hint—if you can't function without coffee, you need more sleep. I know it seems like it's not such a big deal. Most of us take sleep completely for granted and view it, depending on our temperament, as either an all-too-infrequent luxury or a necessary evil that prevents us from working the full twenty-four hours in a day. We, as a culture, are chronically sleep-deprived and inanely proud of it. How many times have you stumbled for the coffeepot and lamely explained, "I was up until four in the morning," as if you deserved some sort of merit badge? Persistent lack of sleep can result in impaired cognitive function, depression, irritability, hypertension, and—horror of horrors—weight gain! If you want to make sure your body is in top performance mode, give it the time it needs for rest and rejuvenation.

Minding Your Matter

Before you get carried away with your cleansing and yoga and power napping, I want to remind you that total wellness isn't just about your body. Your mental state has as much impact on your health as anything you do. Negative responses to stress can elevate blood pressure, weaken your immune system, and contribute to everything from heart disease to digestive problems.

But the power of the mind-body connection can also be harnessed for good. Certainly what has come to be known as the placebo effect has demonstrated that people can overcome disease by merely *believing* they are being treated. Through controlling your emotions with techniques like meditation and biofeedback, you can help yourself heal on every level.

The Body Electric

There is another component in your overall wellness, one that your doctor probably won't check at your next scheduled physical: your *energy*. I'm not talking about your pep or zip, but that underlying vital force that is the very essence of the universe. Now you're wondering. "What could energy possibly have to do with health?" Well, the short answer is, Everything! Life is defined by energy. It's the difference between a tree and a wooden chair—or a corpse and you or me. At the cellular level, what defines life is the energy gradient of the cell membrane; that's the charge inside the cell in relationship to the charge outside the cell.

I'm sure you're familiar with Einstein's famous equation, $E = mc^2$, stating that all matter is actually energy. Our cultural paradigm explaining the nature of the universe is no longer a purely mechanistic one. Modern physics has taken us beyond Newton's laws. Even high school students understand that what appears to be solid matter is mostly empty space.

Sadly, modern medicine is still mired in its mechanistic/chemically based paradigm and fails to recognize the body as an energetic entity. But many ancient healing traditions of the East are built on this principle and have utilized it to treat people for millennia. Healing systems like acupuncture, Reiki, therapeutic touch, and qigong all seek to redirect or facilitate the flow of energy through the body, thereby improving health.

I'm a certified Reiki master, which sounds like I scratch people with a garden tool at some S & M club, but actually just means that I have learned to focus energy in my own body and to facilitate healing in others. I know it sounds wacky. Trust me, coming from a family of medical doctors (did I mention my brother is a neurosurgeon?), I was skeptical at first. But after I went through the training and began using it on my family and saw the results, I became a believer. Now my kids beg me for it whenever they feel sick.

A Few of My Favorite Things

One of the things I love about most complementary and alternative therapies is that they're holistic. They view the patient as an entire being, in which all systems are related and interdependent. With this approach, specific diseases are seen not as isolated to a particular organ but as symptomatic of a broader imbalance throughout the body. In many of these traditions, effective healing must take place on the emotional and spiritual levels as well as in the body for lasting health to be restored.

There are myriads of these modalities available to the body-conscious and intellectually curious. The following is a list of my absolute, all-time greatest hits. It's by no means comprehensive or exhaustive. If you happen to adore ear candling or crystal therapy and don't see it here, please don't be offended. Also, don't be intimidated if you haven't heard of some of these therapies. The purpose of this section is just to introduce you to the possibility of broadening your healing options. These are the things I use regularly and have found beneficial. By the way, for those of you who won't try anything unless your physician gives it to you, Mehmet uses these therapies too!

Also, be aware that if you look up some of these practices on Wikipedia, you will see phrases like "no proven efficacy." That doesn't mean it doesn't work. It just means that no large pharmaceutical company has funded a randomized, controlled, multimillion-dollar study to demonstrate the treatment's ability to make money. Lack of a patent and a marketing plan does not mean a treatment is worthless. Well, at least not for the patient. Anecdotal evidence may not be enough to get a peer-reviewed article in the *Journal of the American Medical Association*, but when people get results from a therapy—especially when it's been around for thousands of years—I would bet there's something to it. Which brings us to our first modality.

ACUPUNCTURE This is a traditional Chinese healing method that uses needles to stimulate the flow of energy through the body along special pathways or meridians. During the treatment you'll look like a cross between a hedgehog and *Hellraiser II*, but most of the time you can't even feel it. I have had needles in my head, in my face, in my belly, and in my toes. The only place that was slightly uncomfortable being pricked was my shin. I've used acupuncture with great results for back pain, headaches, and wrinkles and have relatives who found it effective with infertility and weight loss.

CRANIOSACRAL THERAPY Here a practitioner very gently and almost imperceptibly manipulates the skull to subtly adjust the cranial bones. I was treated for headaches, which it turns out were caused by an injury I had received ten years earlier. The osteopath could tell exactly where I had hit my head and, by using slight pressure, was able to take away the pain entirely.

AROMATHERAPY Essential oils can be used either directly on the skin or inhaled through the nose. They are believed to treat both physical and emotional ailments. Our family uses them all the time for everything from flu symptoms to skin irritations. I've found lavender to be calming and incredibly effective for burns. Mehmet likes tea tree oil for minor infections.

MASSAGE Who doesn't like a massage? I can't say enough good things about this wonderfully relaxing, stress-relieving, healing technique. And it's not just about chilling out for an hour at the spa (though isn't that justification enough?). Massage is actually great for stimulating lymphatic drainage, which is your body's internal detoxification system.

REFLEXOLOGY This is sort of like massage, but it's just for your feet. (Occasionally it is also used on the hands or ears.) The theory is that different areas on the feet represent the different regions of the body. For example, the head is roughly the toe area. The spine is the outer edge of the foot. The reproductive organs are in the heel, and so on. If you're in good health, it feels awesome. But if you have a problem somewhere in your body, the corresponding location will be quite tender on your foot. You'll want the practitioner to take it easy, but really working the area is what stimulates healing, so embrace the sensation and see how great you feel afterward.

HOMEOPATHY This is my favorite form of "alternative" medicine. In fact, for just about everything except strep throat, this is the first line of treatment in the Oz household. Bruises, scrapes, colds, fevers, nausea, and menstrual cramps are all effectively dealt with using a few tiny sugar pills. The principle behind homeopathy is "Like cures like." So substances that may cause certain symptoms in large doses, for instance arsenic and belladonna, when diluted stimulate the body's immune system to combat those symptoms.

BACH FLOWER REMEDIES These are tinctures made from flower essences that work primarily on emotional states. The one we use most frequently is a blend called Rescue Remedy, and that's exactly what it is. I give it to my kids when they are hurt or having a tantrum, and within seconds the drama is over. It's much easier to deal with a situation once the sobbing has stopped. (It's also good for harried mothers who need to remain calm under pressure.)

CHINESE HERBAL MEDICINE Twigs and leaves and roots and bark—drinking a medicinal tea can seem like you're snacking on the forest floor. And in case you were wondering, that's just what it tastes like. I don't think I have ever had anything with a worse flavor and aroma than the most recent brew I was given by the unfathomably old man in a back room in Chinatown. Drinking a plant potion isn't as crazy as it sounds. Remember, many of our contemporary pharmaceuticals had botanical roots. (Don't you love a bad pun?) Aspirin was originally derived from willow bark and common cardiac drugs from the flower foxglove.

If you're curious about trying any of these modalities, talk to your doctor. You can also find more information and a local practitioner online. Do your research and get references or check with accreditation boards for specialties where they exist. If any therapy makes you feel uncomfortable in any way, discontinue immediately. But keep yourself open to different ways of approaching wellness. You will eventually find your healing path.

Rx for Life

If all this is too much for you to take in, don't worry about it. You want to be healthy, but you don't want to obsess over it. Being preoccupied with your own wellness just makes you self-absorbed, which is death to your relationships. Creating a life full of vitality doesn't have to be all-consuming. Basically, I think it boils down to three things. The first is *awareness*. Total health involves being conscious of what you are doing, why you're doing it, *and* the consequences of those actions. Living on autopilot may help you survive, but it will never get you to thrive. For that you need to make your lifestyle choices with deliberate thought and intention.

The second essential is *action*. You may know what to do, but actually making the change is what counts. The latest health information does nothing to improve your body if it stays in your head.

The third element for health is *purpose*. You need a motivation for what you do—in regard to your health and in life in general. As Mehmet likes to put it, "Give your heart a reason to keep beating."

Wellness can't be the goal in and of itself. Why do you want to be healthy? What's the point of having a strong, fit body if it isn't used for something worthwhile? Be well so you can be of greater service, so you can love more completely, and so you can fulfill that destiny which is uniquely yours.

EXERCISE

Healthy Habits

The exercise for this week is to try to live as healthfully as possible for seven days. It's really not that hard, and you might find you actually prefer it. If not, you can go back to your old wicked ways.

DAY 1. This is the food part. Starting today and throughout the rest of the week, cut out anything that you don't in your heart (or gut) feel is health-sustaining. There are no hard-and-fast rules. I'm not telling you what you can or can't have. You're the boss of you. But please don't lie to yourself. No BS rationalizing, like "There's calcium in that ice cream, so it's good for me." Ask your body if the food will provide the nourishment it needs. By the way, the tongue doesn't count as part of your body on this one. It's not to be trusted.

DAY 2. Incorporate movement into your day. Wake up ten minutes early so you can stretch. I like the yoga "sun salutation." Start by standing with your feet together and your hands at your sides. Reach up toward the sky, gaze upward, and lean back a little as you inhale, then lean forward exhaling and place your hands on the ground in front of you (bending your knees if you need to). Jump or step your feet back behind you, keeping your hands on the floor. On an inhalation drop your hips, arch your back and look upward. Then exhale and push your hips upward. Relax your neck and shoulders. Hold this position for a few breaths. Finally look forward and step or jump your feet back to standing position.

I repeat this cycle around three times to get all my muscles warmed up, but you can use any series of stretches you prefer. Remember to create movement in all directions—up, down, side to side. And be sure to get the upper and lower parts of your body. Your muscles are all connected to each other, so tight hamstrings can result in a stiff back and twisting your ankle can end up affecting your hip. Try not to hold your breath at any point. Do this every morning for the rest of the week.

DAY 3. Speaking of breathing, today you're going to add conscious breathing to your healthy week activities. Start by breathing normally. Place a hand on your belly, just above your navel, and notice if your hand is floating gently up and down. If not, you're not engaging your diaphragm. So this time as you inhale, keep your chest still and imagine the air filling your abdomen. Make sure your stomach is soft so that it can rise as you inhale and drop as you exhale. Continue this deep diaphragmatic breathing for ten minutes and repeat every day for the rest of the week.

DAY 4. You're going to expand on the breath work by adding alternate-nostril breathing. Place the thumb of your right hand by your right nostril and your right ring finger next to your left nostril. Curl your middle two fingers down and out of the way. Gently close the right nostril by pressing it with your thumb as you inhale through the left nostril. Then close the left nostril with your ring finger, as you release your right nostril .

and slowly exhale. Inhale through the right nostril, then switch, closing the right and releasing the left to exhale. Then inhale through the left and exhale right. Do this for five minutes after you have completed the ten minutes of deep breathing. If you can't just chill and breathe for fifteen minutes, you can cut it down to ten minutes a day. If you can't find that in your calendar, you've got some serious time management issues.

DAY 5. If you're not what you'd call an exerciser, start by just walking. On this day and for the next two, try to walk as much as possible. If you can schedule in half an hour or more to jump on a treadmill or briskly stride around the neighborhood park, by all means do it! If not, then opt to take the stairs at work, park at the far end of the lot, and march in place through your favorite sitcom. Before you go to bed, do ten push-ups (they can be the girl version) and twenty crunches. If you're already hitting the gym on a regular basis, use these few days to push yourself a little bit further than your regular routine. Go the extra mile, and I mean literally.

DAY 6. Get in touch with your energetic flow. When you first wake up, right before you get out of bed, take your hands and place them in a prayer position about six inches away from your heart. Rub them together briskly for a few seconds just to get the blood flowing and then separate them by about an inch. Close your eyes and see if you can sense an energy field between the hands. Now place them over your face without actually touching it. Again, see if you can feel anything. Finally, place one hand on top of the other and hold them just over your heart, still about an inch away. Envision the love and gratitude you have for your physical being manifested as pure energy radiating from your hands and pouring into your chest.

See the energy as a golden light that spreads to include your whole body. Drop your hands, open your eyes, and take that loving energy out into the world as you begin your day.

DAY 7. Today you're going to do all the things you've been doing earlier in the week, but you're also going to find an extra few minutes when you can quietly sit down with a pen and paper and write your "reasons to thrive" list. Draw a line down the middle of the paper, and on the left side write all the things you could do better if you were fit and strong and optimally healthy. Include things that are purely personal, like "I could run a marathon," and things that involve your loved ones, like "I would be a better role model for my daughter." End with one that is more spiritual, like "I would be honoring this body as an awesome gift from God and treating it in a way that shows my gratitude daily."

CHAPTER 5

You Again

∞

O kay, now we get to the juicy stuff. This is where we actually talk about relationships. (Well, I'll talk about mine and you can extrapolate to yours.) And no, this isn't the sexy part yet. We'll get to that. But first I thought it would be useful to go over the ways we interact with people in general. We are in continual association with others (at least those of us who aren't practicing hermits). It is through our relationships that we demonstrate who we are. This is where our character is revealed. Thomas Merton says, "We cannot find ourselves within ourselves, but only in others, yet at the same time before we can go out to others we must first find ourselves." Sounds a little confusing, but the point is that who we are is determined in large part by our relationships. The profound role that many of them play is obvious. Parents, teachers, lovers, and enemies all impact us directly. But there's not a single interaction with another person that doesn't influence us in some way.

I believe that there are no coincidences. Everything in life exists for a reason. This principle has been expressed as fate, karma, kismet, synchronicity, and destiny. Swedenborg calls it Divine Providence, which is fundamentally the idea that our lives are being directed in a way that is most beneficial for our spiritual evolution while still allowing us the freedom to choose good or evil. If we accept this to be the case, then we must acknowledge that the people we encounter are part of this process. There is a purpose to the relationship—for both them and us. Our connection provides the catalyst for personal growth.

Life is a series of learning experiences, and many of its lessons come in the form of human interactions. Most of us think that the relationships that are pleasurable are the blessings in our lives and that those with people who are cruel or harsh or merely unpleasant are unnecessary at best. But every single person we come in contact with provides a unique opportunity for our inner self to either evolve or degenerate. Relationships, especially those driven by conflict, push us outside our comfort zone. Often the principles taught by these encounters are the ones that would be hard for us to grasp on our own—things like forgiveness, humility, and compassion. So in the big picture, even "bad" relationships can be good. But in general, the better our relationships are, the more we will enjoy the ride.

Do Unto Others

Since the nature of our interactions with others pretty much determines the quality of our experience, it would seem to be in our best interest to make these relationships as good as possible. Of course, *good* is a relative term. Some of you might interpret this to mean that I think you should only hang out with the super pious.

To others, it could seem like I'm recommending friends who are loads of fun. That's not what I'm talking about. I'm sure you have people in your life who are naughty or boring or both. And I certainly wouldn't want you to cut them off. (Well, maybe just the boring ones.) But what I mean by a good relationship is one that is approached consciously; the participants behave in a manner that is congruent with their values. This is the type of relationship that is mutually beneficial and satisfying, based on kindness and compassion.

And by the way, this is what we strive for not only with our soul mate or favorite aunt, but also with our chief competition at work and the quasi-sadistic meter maid who writes up a ticket while you're searching the bottom of your purse for a quarter. Ideally, we would approach every encounter with a sense of presence and awareness. Note I said "ideally." It's not going to happen all the time (it certainly doesn't with me). But it's not an unreasonable goal. And it's nothing new.

What I'm talking about is fundamentally the Golden Rule—roughly, "Treat others the way you would want them to treat you." It's about realizing that the world isn't centered on what we want at any given moment and showing us that our behavior has ramifications. Without any ambiguity, it tells us that we are responsible for our actions because we know their impact—based on our own likes and dislikes. It's very clever in its absolute clarity and simplicity. If something would feel bad for me, of course it would feel bad for you too, so I really shouldn't do it. It makes perfect sense. And it seems so easy—almost too easy.

Ha! Try actually doing it! To stop and ask, "What would I want if I were that person?" before you do something to somebody is ridiculously hard. When I manage to broach the question, I can get into a dizzying dialogue of justification and validation that leads nowhere. "Well, if I were him, what I really would want is for the other person to be happy, so then I should do it. Plus I know that he knows that I know, so then I would definitely want me to do it . . ." Insanity. Talk enough and you can rationalize anything. Also, it's so much easier to apply the rule to the big, theoretical, "never going to happen anyway" stuff—like, "I wouldn't want him to steal my car, so I won't take his." It's in the subtle, everyday interactions that it starts to get messy.

For example, I have an ugly tendency to gossip. And I'm good at it. I can weave a tale, add humor, and build to the punch line. I am a gossip maestro. And I enjoy it, in the same way as I enjoy eating condensed milk off a spoon. (They're both tasty but make me feel slightly ill afterward.) A gossip fest would seem like the perfect opportunity to practice the "Do unto others as you would have them do unto you" philosophy of life. It's certainly the sort of thing I don't want other people to do to me! But once you start, it takes a lot to reverse the momentum.

Which is why I was so grateful for my gossiper/gossipee experience. A while back I was visiting an aesthetician, whom I love. We always reconnect by exchanging pleasantries. Then, once I've disrobed and mounted her paper-covered table, we begin to dish. The stories help us both ignore the fact that she's tearing hair out of very sensitive regions. On this particular occasion the wax was unusually hot and the tale especially juicy. I was recounting a rumor about a woman we both knew when she interrupted and said, "Oh, you know, I have this one client who . . . ," and proceeded to tell me an embarrassing story about *me*! It was something from a few years earlier and she had obviously forgotten that I was the person involved. But I hadn't. And I was mortified. How many other people had she told? I faked a snicker at the part I knew was supposed to be funny, but it must have sounded off because she added quickly, "I'm sorry, you were in the middle of telling me something." I winced, partly in pain from the most recent rip, and partly because the last thing in the world I wanted to do was continue with my narrative. I wrapped it up quickly, muttering something about everything turning out fine, pulled on my sweatpants, and skulked out like a chastened dog.

I love irony. It's like a laugh and a wink from God. And this was one of those cosmic gotchas that I can't resist. I'd been given a relatively painless (in spite of the depilation) opportunity to experience firsthand exactly what I was doing to someone else. It was more than empathy. It was like a momentary merging of selves. At the same instant I was the victim and the perpetrator. I totally got the Golden Rule. Does that mean I practice it? Sometimes. I still like a good story, but not as much, and not without an inner cringe of knowing what it feels like to be on the other side.

Intention Reads

If we all lived by doing what we would want the other person to do—even part of the time—we would all get along much better. But sometimes you can ruin a relationship without doing anything at all. Sometimes it's not what you do that creates a negative interaction, but what you're thinking.

A lifetime ago, back when I was studying acting, I ended up with a second brilliant but grouchy teacher. (Are there any jolly ones out there?) His lessons were useful for improving our nascent theatrical technique, but invaluable when applied to life in general. I remember one afternoon when two young men were doing a scene from a contemporary play in which they were supposed to be close friends. The teacher interrupted them a few lines in and asked them to think about the words and start again. They had barely begun their exchange when he made them repeat it, urging them to actually *mean* what they said.

This was painful (yes, worse than a bikini wax). Watching the scene had been bad, but watching it over and over was torture. The forced smiles and feigned sincerity as the two men struggled to communicate their emotions were quickly turning what was supposed to be a poignant drama into a macabre comedy. I had no idea where the teacher was going with this, yet he seemed pleased with the downward direction.

Finally, he made them stop. "Marc," he asked bluntly, "what do you think of Evan?"

"Of his character in the play?" Marc seemed puzzled.

"No, him as a person."

Marc opened his mouth but nothing came out. You know the old "If you can't say anything nice" rule . . .

"You don't like him, do you?" said the teacher, upping the awkwardness quotient in the room by about 300 percent.

"I guess not," Marc replied, concentrating on a coffee mark on his script in order to avoid eye contact.

"It reads," said the teacher matter-of-factly. "You can say whatever words you like, but the message we're all getting loud and clear is that you think he's a prick."

Someone in the class laughed nervously and the teacher turned his attention to those of us who were not performing. "It always reads. Remember that."

There are so many places where it's important to keep this in mind. My own personal favorites are cocktail parties and parent-teacher conferences. I've noticed that in both situations I can grin and nod till my head wobbles off, but if what I'm thinking is "Get me the heck out of here," then that is the message I'm sending.

Most people are so caught up in their own thoughts and dialogue that they aren't entirely aware of what they or others are projecting. That's how we all get away with it so frequently. Still, there are many encounters where there's no overt altercation yet both parties end up feeling embittered. That's because the nonverbal signals you send are determined by what's going on in your mind, not what's coming out of your mouth. So what do you do?

Well, my acting teacher had a very innovative solution. "Marc, find something you like about Evan," he suggested.

"Anything?" Marc asked.

"Anything at all."

Marc gave Evan the once-over and offered, "I guess his shirt's okay."

Not much to work with, but my teacher had been doing this for twenty-five years. Nothing fazed him. "Fine. We'll focus on the shirt. I want you to really get into that shirt and everything about it that totally works on Evan. See how the fabric hangs gently from his shoulders. Notice how the color complements his eyes. Look at how precise the stitching is. And when you know in your heart that that is the perfect shirt for Evan, then start the scene."

It was crazy, but the technique actually worked. Admittedly, neither of them was going to win a Tony any time soon, but what they said was believable. The change in focus had shifted the energy of the scene. And it works in real life. Now, I'm not suggesting this as some crazy manipulative tool to make a person like you or to trick them into thinking you like them. But I find that when I'm the most judgmental, my interactions are the worst. When I let go of my negative thoughts and can find something I like in the other person or in our relationship, not only do I enjoy the exchange more, but the outcome is generally more positive.

A few years back I had a rather awkward working relationship with a woman I wasn't crazy about. We were involved in a film project together and didn't share a single opinion on the direction the movie should take. I was thinking epic adventure and somewhere in the back of her mind I'm sure she was picturing a movie of the week. It got to the point where I would sit through meetings counting the minutes until I could run back to another partner and report on how irritating she was.

One day I came to the office and her boss said this woman was dropping off the team. I refrained from doing a jig of glee right there in the reception area and decided instead to say good-bye to her. I knocked on her door and poked my head in. "Hey, I just wanted to let you know how sorry I am not to be working with you," I lied. "Me too," she lied back. "What are you going to be doing?" I asked just to be polite. "Well, I'm going to scale back a bit and spend some more time riding."

It turns out she was an expert equestrian. I grew up with horses, so I can totally relate to anyone who wants to spend more time with them. We spent half an hour chatting about her upcoming competitions and bonded over a mutual love of jumping. By the time I left, she had decided to stay peripherally involved in our film. And while I still tended to disagree with her notes, I actually ended up looking forward to our interactions.

The point of this story is not to imply that your current nemesis can or should be your best friend. While it would be lovely if we could get along with everyone all the time, I'm pretty sure it can't be done. And I'm not sure I'd want to. I don't think conflict is always a bad thing. Differences of opinion push us outside our comfort zone. Conflict can teach us new ways of seeing situations or clarify and solidify our commitment to our own perspective. It's in our fights that we test our mettle, where we see what we're capable of, where we find our limits.

Plus, there are a lot of bad people with whom you don't want to agree anyway. Some folks are just horrible. I know that's a politically incorrect thing to say. The relativists of the world will assert that *bad* is a subjective term, and the New Agers will tell you that in reality we're all good and there's no such thing as evil. At the risk of offending them, I'm going to state for the record that I think that's a crock. As long as there are genocides and child pornography, I'm holding to the notion that there are people worth fighting.

That being said, there are ways to be in productive conflict and ways that will drag you back to pre-Neanderthal stages of emotional development. I personally have run the gamut of pugilist styles and can attest to the ineffectualness of blame, shame, passive aggression, and guilt. There are, however, a few things that I have found useful to keep in mind during an altercation.

Don't Go Changing (Someone Else)

The first is to realize that you can't change anyone else. The horrible truth is that people just don't do what you want them to. Frankly, sometimes it seems like they're deliberately trying to thwart you. Sometimes with direct, honest dialogue you can help them to see things differently. Sometimes with threats you can create a scenario they'll want less than the original one. But the bottom line is that you can't *make* them do anything. The only thing you can control in any conflict is yourself, and that's on a really good day.

I have about three perfect friendships. We never fight. Nothing they do bugs me. I have no desire to change them in any way. This is not true for everyone else in my life. Especially not the people I love most. My parents treat me like a large child, my kids talk back, and my husband patently refuses to come home for dinner.

My typical response is generally anger, frustration, occasionally rage. Not a happy state. But the negative emotion is almost always justified. I have every right to be mad when dinner's been on the table so long it's growing mold and the children are gnawing on their knuckles in hunger by the time Mehmet saunters through the door. Right? Maybe.

I don't really like being mad. For one thing I tend to eat when I get mad and that makes me fat and fat makes me even madder. So, in the interest of my waistline, I decide to fix things. I know if I can just get Mehmet to come home on time, everyone will be happy. I determine to show him the error of his ways in a logical, compelling manner. I sit him down and discuss why it is important that he be home within several hours of his professed ETA. The children have school and can't be up until midnight, eating late is bad for your metabolism, fourteen hours each day should be plenty of time to get his work done, yada, yada, yada. I am calm, collected, direct. He sees my point, understands the error of his ways, and promises that he will be home by 7:30 the following evening.

Fast-forward to the next night. It's 9:45. Where's Mehmet? Not home. Admittedly he's not out drinking with the guys. Maybe he got out of the OR late, or he had a last-minute conference call with the president of Turkey, or he had to spell-check the final draft of his next book. There's a good reason he's not here. It's just not good enough for me. He broke a promise. I'm ticked off.

This time, instead of the composed, thoughtful conversation, when he walks through the door I blast him. I'm a good yeller. And I can always work in some mean, spiteful little phrases. By the time I'm done, the children have run for cover and Mehmet has declared that he didn't want dinner anyway and stormed off to finish his emails. This technique is clearly not working.

I move on to bribery—sex on the nights he makes it home for dinner. Threats—no sex if he's late. Compromise is no solution. "You come home late tonight, then early tomorrow." But of course tomorrow is always a day away. Sulking, the silent treatment, physical punishment in the form of my latest kung fu grip—all have the same impact: none. And lest you imagine that my husband is uniquely intransigent, let me assure you, his spawn are equally stubborn. My daughter Zoe is physically incapable of turning off a light. It's almost as if her fingers can't perform the downward flick.

Once she's walked through an area, it will blaze brighter than the noonday sun until someone else (yes, that means me) goes by and turns everything off. Again, no amount of cajoling, threatening, or rationalizing can get her to change her ways.

Since my daughter is only fifteen and I still have some influence on her behavior, I am hopeful that by the time she leaves for college she will at least be able to use a dimmer, but my husband is another case altogether. Because I've been so sure that I am right in this situation and that Mehmet is just being pigheaded, I always figured that if I were persistent, creative, or convincing enough, he would eventually come around. But after almost twenty-five years of marriage I'm beginning to realize that the next ice age may well be upon us before he comes home early on any kind of a regular basis. And the sad fact is that short of dragging him out of his office and driving him home myself, there's not a damn thing I can do about it.

This being the case, it may seem that I'm destined for a life of cold dinners and tired children. But there's another possibility. I have resisted it for decades but out of sheer exhaustion am beginning to think it may be the best option. In this new dinnertime world, the children and I eat, they finish their homework, and occasionally go to bed well before Mehmet walks through the door. This is a scenario in which I get what I want, mostly. But it's also a scenario in which I have to give up the very deep-seated desire to control another person.

As I mentioned earlier, one of the fundamental truths of just about every human interaction is that we *can't change other people.* This is a tough one. We all think if we can just get our spouse, parent, boss, friendly IRS agent to see the situation from our perspective—or we can make the repercussions of their behavior painful enough, or we can manipulate them into feeling guilty—then they will stop doing whatever it is that's driving us crazy, and everything will be fine.

Maybe you don't behave this way. Maybe you couldn't give a rat's whisker about anyone else's choices. If so, I applaud you. You are highly evolved and are probably a monk who doesn't speak to other people anyway. But if you're anything like me, this is an ongoing source of frustration in just about every relationship. It is not, however, a hopeless situation. For a mere $19.99, you too can purchase the "zap collar" . . . Not really. But don't think it wasn't on my list. Sadly, the only real solution lies in modifying your own behavior.

I can hear the collective "Hell no, they're the ones who need to change!" And I know where you're coming from. But unless you want to wait twenty years to find out for yourself, believe me when I assure you: it's not going to happen. Or at least you're not going to make it happen. Once this truth sets in, and you realize you're not the king of the universe and cannot make everyone else do your bidding, as sensible and benevolent as it might be, the question of "Now what?" arises.

For me it became clear that what I needed to do was let go of my need to blame someone else and then be really honest with myself—about myself—acknowledging the fact that my behavior was partly responsible for the situation. You're rolling your eyes. I know, it sounds so dignified and removed and holier-than-thou. However, my realization of personal responsibility was anything but.

On about the seven hundredth time Mehmet came home late I had my epiphany—and not in a flashing lights and music kind of way but in the cold, hard, hit-you-in-the-face-with-a-fish style that epiphanies often resort to. I had sliced my finger mincing the onions for Mehmet's favorite sautéed mushrooms, burnt the tofu turkey, and already screamed at the kids several times before the phone rang at 8:15. "I'm leaving in about twenty minutes," said the familiar voice at the other end. "Fine," I responded. But what

I was really thinking was "Could I have the locks changed before he gets home?" I kicked over the chair by the phone, shoveled the mushrooms into the garbage pail, and was in the process of stuffing the tofu in after them when my youngest at the time tiptoed into the room. "I'm hungry," she chirped. I quickly retracted the pan with the tofu turkey and slid it across the counter. "There." She glanced at the food. "I need a fork." I was about to tell her to get it herself when she followed with "And I think you need a time-out."

Wow. That was harsh. And accurate. I resisted the urge to wash her mouth out with soap for being rude and hurried off to the closest bathroom, where I slammed the door and promptly assumed the "ball on the floor" position.

Time-outs are wonderful things. They are useful on so many levels. I love that they are flexible, in terms of both where and how long. They can be used on toddlers and teenagers and, in this case, even moms. They require neither yelling nor rationalizing, and whether or not they're an effective deterrent for the next round of bad behavior, they are an extremely effective method of interrupting the pattern at that moment.

I lay on the cold tile and thought about my predicament. I allowed several minutes of the obligatory "Oh, my miserable fate" tirade to run through my head. I was overworked, unappreciated, mistreated, undervalued, and a few other pitiful adjectives that were untrue but added color. I let myself rant until I was tuckered out. I paused for a second, and a little voice in my head blurted, "Anything else?" This was not the voice that had been whining. How I had two voices in my head was beyond me. For a second I wondered if schizophrenia ran back in some forgotten part of my family tree that no one had bothered to fill me in on. But there was that question, hanging over me like a cartoon bubble. I thought about it for a bit. "Well yes, there is something else. He's so incredibly selfish!" "Let's keep this about you, shall we?" the second voice interrupted. If I had a split personality, one of them was very bossy. "Just about me? He's the big fat jackass in this situation." "So fine, he's a jackass. What about you?" That voice was really starting to get on my nerves. But what about me? Certainly I was the innocent, kitchen-weary victim in all this. Wasn't I? I was about to counter with something snappy to this effect but decided to just shut up for a moment and give both voices a rest. I allowed myself to be still.

In this place of quiet I was able to detach from the situation. Remember the observation exercise we talked about in the first chapter, and the peace I found from the focused breathing in the section on suffering? Sometimes it happens spontaneously. Once I had let go of the need to control/change my husband, and I took my brain out of judgment mode, I could see what I was doing.

What Do You Want—Really?

We all play a role in our conflicts. At some point we need to take responsibility for that. Once we do, we give ourselves the power to break the pattern. My response of impotent rage was as much a part of our domestic dance as Mehmet's obtuse stubbornness. When I admitted that I was a participant in the ongoing argument, I actually felt better. There was something I could do. I hadn't been able to change Mehmet, but I could change myself.

To decide where and how to change, I had to ask some more questions. (You'll get used to the voice in your head too, after a while.) What exactly was I doing that was contributing to the problem? When you pose this question to yourself, try to answer it from the other person's point of view. If you were to ask this person, what would he or she say you are doing? In Mehmet's mind I was setting up unrealistic expectations, blowing things out of proportion, nagging him, and undermining his relationship with the children by yelling at him in front of them.

So that's what I was doing. Looking at the list in retrospect, it's pretty obvious that none of those things was going to bring him home any earlier. But it's hard to just stop doing something (even if it's not working) when you don't know the real reasons you're doing it. So the next question to ask was "Why am I making these choices?" When you phrase it like that, you remind yourself that you are the author of your behavior, you are not a victim of circumstance. Also, it's a far more effective question than "What do you want?" because the only answer that ever comes up for that one is "To get the other person to change!"

Now, this is where it gets a bit tricky. We all initially respond to that question with the really obvious stuff. For me, it would have been "Because the kids need to eat dinner and go to bed blah blah blah"—reasons I gave before. But the surface answers are never the real answers. It's imperative that you be totally honest with yourself here. At least as much as you can be. I'm a good bullshitter, and I bet you're not so bad at it either. But when we bullshit ourselves, we're losing an opportunity to go deeper and get to know who we really are. One of the things I had to face honestly in this situation was that Mehmet wasn't keeping our kids up too late or keeping them from eating. I was. I could have put them to bed at five in the afternoon if I'd felt like it, but I chose to keep them up as part of my arsenal to manipulate my husband.

Once that was off the table, I had to look at my real motivation. Well, truth be told, I was lonely. I was bored. I love my kids, but sometimes I need adult companionship. Mehmet was having fun at the hospital and I was just counting down the minutes until he got home to play with me. When he did get home—invariably late— neither of us was in any mood for playing.

Time to go to the next level. What was it that I was expressing through my frustration at his tardiness? Way deep down in those places I like to ignore, I was feeling a little resentful that he was fulfilling his dreams, interacting with his peers, and learning something new every day, while the only thing I was learning was that pureed broccoli is uniformly rejected by children and green cleaning products really do work just as well as harsh chemicals for average household needs. (Such thrilling information. I bet you're enthralled just reading about it.) I felt stagnant and unproductive, and somehow thought that would be cured if our family could eat a single meal together before the sun went down. What that act represented in my mind was that my husband valued what I was doing.

The real problem was that *I* didn't value what I was doing. I was neither stimulated nor satisfied by being a stay-at-home mom. What I needed to do was either change how I felt or change what I was doing. I ended up doing both.

First, I found something I could do while raising the children that would challenge me and provide the sense of creative expression that I craved. I began writing screenplays while the kids were in school or napping or at the playground with the babysitter. And then I determined to be more fully engaged when I was with them. I gave mothering more meaning for myself by actively participating in the process rather than just going through the motions. Ironically, even the dullest tasks become more enjoyable when you are more fully present and aware.

Now you may be wondering, "What's the takeaway from that rather long story about a temper tantrum over burnt tofu?" Well, I don't think a long, in-depth self-therapy session is practical with every interaction, but there are a few key insights that are broadly applicable. To start is the idea of genuine presence. One of my favorite quotes is "Wherever you go, there you are" from the movie *Buckaroo Banzai*. It has that delicious quality of being totally silly and shockingly profound at the same time. Realizing this fact and living it is probably the single most important thing we can do to improve our relationships. Far too often we are physically with a person but our head's someplace else. Whether we're on the phone, listening to the radio, watching TV, or just caught up in our own thoughts, when we are not present in the moment—with the people next to us—we cheat ourselves and them of an opportunity to make a real connection.

Another important lesson is the necessity of practicing self-awareness, especially during conflict. The next time you find yourself in an argument, ask yourself what you really want and how your behavior is helping to meet those needs. The answer might not come to you during the heat of passion, but at some point before you make yourself and someone else miserable, take a moment to create a safe place where you can be really honest with yourself. Once you have a clue about why you are choosing certain actions, see what changes you can implement to achieve your goals, regardless of what the other person is doing. Remember, it's all really about you.

Except in my case, where it's all really about me. And since we're on me, I bet you're wondering how my getting-home-late fight turned out. What exactly changed thanks to all that drama and introspection? Frankly, not much—except my attitude. Mehmet still comes home late. Often later than he used to. But I no longer want to hurl something at him when he arrives, and usually the kids have been fed. The situation is similar but I am different, so it's no longer an issue.

Get Higher

Ultimately what we seek with each other is connection—not at the base ego level where we spend most of our time, but in that core space that makes us human. This is the type of union that always seeks the higher good; that lives in Christ's second great commandment to love our neighbor as ourselves. There's a Sanskrit word Mehmet and I learned in yoga class that pretty much embodies within a single word this ideal of living in relationship. *Namaste* means "the divine in me honors the divine in you." It is a recognition of the sacred within both ourselves and others, and speaks to the fact that we are equals; we are from God and we are here to love one another. *Namaste*, my friend. *Namaste*.

Loving Your Neighbor

DAY 1. This is a game called "the hiding Buddha" that my mother made up after reading a tale in which the Buddha comes into the life of a monk disguised as his adversary. It's a way of internally shifting negative thoughts about someone into a moment of self-reflection and gratitude. The point is that no matter how much of a jerk someone is, he or she can still provide you with the opportunity for personal growth. Remember, your journey is not about making that person less of a jerk; it's always and only about you.

So, here's what you do. The next time someone does something that gets you mad, imagine that she didn't actually *want* to do it but her Buddha-self accepted the task in order to help you reach enlightenment. Imagine that under her mean or stupid behavior is a smiling Buddha, who only wishes the best for you. See where you are being stretched or tested in this situation, where you can choose to act from your higher self. Say an inner thank-you and acknowledge how unpleasant it must be for her to have to act in such an obnoxious way.

Then take on the challenge of responding with compassion and gratitude.

DAY 2. The next time you find yourself in an ongoing argument with someone, try switching sides. You give all the reasons he's right and have him defend your position. For example, if your teenager wants to go to a party on Saturday night, let her demonstrate why this is a terrible idea, and you try to convince her that it is perfectly acceptable. See if you make any points with which you both actually agree. Create a resolution from the areas of overlap.

DAY 3. Take inventory of your relationships. List the good ones, the mediocre ones, and the ones that you, frankly, could do without. Beside each one, write down the ways in which you have grown or reacted poorly because of it. If you find that the relationship has had a negative impact on your personal and spiritual development, resolve either to bless it and put it in the past, moving on without resentment, or to improve it by changing yourself.

DAY 4. Remember that in the introduction I said that what I needed to do to learn life's lessons was "show up, be willing to do the work, and be honest with myself and others"? Well, today you're going to start with the first part. You're going to make the effort to show up wherever you are. Really try to be focused on whatever you are experiencing at any given moment, whether it's talking on the phone or mopping your floor. Refuse to multitask. If you are with someone, be present to *that person*. If you are alone, be fully aware of yourself. Do not be distracted by the past or future. Commit to being present in the present.

DAY 5. Today's exercise is to be brutally honest. That means no fudging. So if you're late for your dentist, don't say, "The traffic was horrific," unless it really was. Don't exaggerate. Don't imply something that you don't know for a fact to be accurate, and especially don't make up justifications for yourself. This exercise sounds simple, but it is actually very tough. When you start to notice all the ways you bend the truth, you will be shocked.

DAY 6. It's time to do the work. Think of a situation in which you have been trying to get someone else to change. Fuss as much as you need to and then realize that it will never happen. Now that that's off the table, brainstorm some ways that you could change yourself to improve the relationship. Start with specific things you could do differently, then move on to ways you could think differently by changing your focus, and finally see where you could feel differently through creating new meaning for your experience. The relationship cannot remain static once you have committed to growth.

DAY 7. For one day, try to be aware of how you are connecting with people. Are you supporting the best part of them by offering the best part of yourself, or are you interacting at a base level? Are you bonding with one individual by shutting others out? Are you making yourself feel better by putting someone else down? Are you encouraging another's negativity in order to indulge your own? Notice how even the most subtle of interactions has an intention. Attempt to keep that intention one that comes from a place of love and integrity.

CHAPTER 6

Sexual Union

S ex. There, I said it. Now, let's just get past any awkwardness
that accompanies that word, because I'm going to be using
it a lot. This chapter is about your sexual relationship—your
deepest, most powerful connection to another human being. There
is nothing on earth that can take you higher or lower, nothing else
that can crack you open and show you your own soul through the
mirror of another. Sexuality at its best is about getting access to the
core—the core of yourself, of another person, and of the very universe itself. The fundamental reality of all creation is symbolized
in the act of sex.

I know a bunch of you probably feel I'm verging on hyperbole
here. When I start claiming that the *core of the universe* and the *fundamental reality of creation* are primarily erotic in nature, I tend to
raise a few eyebrows. But I don't think we really have a clue about
how powerful sex actually is.

Our culture is supersaturated with sexual language and images. We're familiar with every anatomical location and function. We have sexual aids and enhancers: pills and films and buzzing things. We have sex all the time with anyone we want, and if we're feeling antisocial, we can approximate it with a computer. You'd think we'd know all about sex. But it's sort of like saying we understand music because we like to play Rock Band or Guitar Hero. You can have a lot of something and not really know it at all.

In my opinion, the problem with sex today is that we have attempted to amputate the innate sensual pleasure from the act of spiritual union, very much in the same way that we have succeeded in isolating enjoyable taste from food, whose primary function is to nourish our bodies. Ironically, while both junk food and casual, commitment-free sex seem appealing, they end up being highly unsatisfying. No one is energized by a bag of puffs or is fulfilled by a meaningless sexual encounter. Both can taste good at the time. Both can become highly addictive. But neither really gives you what you need.

It's one of the strange and wonderful aspects of the nondualistic universe that everything embodies its opposite. Those things that are really powerful in a good way have the potential to be corrupted into a force of terrible darkness. This is especially true of sex, even within marriage. When it's used as a method of controlling others or of obtaining security, sex is rendered incapable of conjoining spirit. If it is nothing more than a way to indulge an urge—a response to lust rather than the longing of the heart—then sex can become harmful and degrading.

I think the real purpose of sex is not to propagate the species, as some biologists will tell you, or even to have fun, as you hedonists might hope, but the joining of souls. It is during sex that we, as natural beings, are most able to transcend space and time, to fully experience our physical bodies and yet identify with that part of ourselves that is distinctly nonmaterial. Our sexual relationships are an attempt to move beyond the boundaries of the ego. They take us to a place where we can break through our isolation and fall into the reality of unity. When we connect on this level, we are able to merge with another so that we are no longer two separate beings but one entity.

Sex is a big deal. Through it, you connect with another being on far more than just the physical level. And in spite of the fact that you can't remember the name of the guy from the bar last Friday, there is no such thing as "meaningless sex." It may not mean as much after just one night as after fifty years, but it's never nothing. When you have sex with someone, it's sort of like a psychic tattoo. Covering it up is fairly easy, but trying to take it off can be painful and expensive. (I'm talking emotional currency here, not cash.) So I recommend you choose your sexual partners wisely.

Love at First Sight

I knew I would marry Mehmet the moment I saw him. It was surreal. You've heard about how people see their lives flash before their eyes right before they die? Well, this was sort of like that— only forward, not backward. You could call it love at first sight, but the sensation was very different from the typical feeling of love. It was more like recognition of destiny. And anyway, it wasn't really first sight. I had met him six months earlier in France, sort of . . .

The summer I was eighteen, I stayed with a warm and gracious family who lived just outside of Lyon. They had a vacation home in a darling little town in the French Alps, where we spent a week. I don't know if it was the altitude that affected me, but each night we were there, I dreamed about a young man with dark hair, green eyes, and a generous smile. I knew he was my future husband, except that it felt like we were already connected in a way far deeper even than marriage—like we'd always been part of each other. The dreams continued the whole time we were in the mountains, then stopped abruptly as soon as we returned to the city. I tried to bring them back, concentrating on the memories of previous nights just before I fell asleep, but it didn't work. Eventually, I came back to the States and forgot all about them.

The following February I joined my parents for dinner with another surgeon and his family. I was running late, so by the time I got to the restaurant, everyone was seated. I spotted their table and decided to bypass the hostess and walk over myself when I felt a hand on my shoulder and a man's voice asked, "May I help you with your coat?" I turned to thank him and was suddenly staring into the eyes of my dream boy—both literally and figuratively. Instantly I recognized every feature, knew the sound of his voice. Even the sensation of his hand on my back was familiar. Oddly, at that moment my only thought was "Wow, how do I tell my parents I'm going to marry the waiter? Maybe he's the maitre d'?"

I fumbled out of my jacket and stood frozen in the center of the room while he took it to the coat-check girl and came back with my ticket. I had no desire to sit down, preferring to follow him into the kitchen, but he proceeded to my parents' table and pulled out my chair. I obediently took my seat, secretly resolving to ask numerous detailed questions about each of the specials.

And then the unfathomable occurred. He sat down next to me. It must have taken a full thirty seconds for me to comprehend that he was a member of our dinner party and not some overly friendly restaurant employee. I blushed, stammered an introduction as I awkwardly shook his hand, and, in a cloud of embarrassment, greeted the rest of our group.

The remainder of the evening proceeded rather uneventfully. Mehmet, though seated next to me, spent most of the time debating the merits of rock music with my mother. Our one interaction was when I offered him my duck canapé, explaining that I was a vegetarian. He was intrigued—in the same way he might have been if I had said I was a pygmy from Papua New Guinea. He ate the appetizer and continued defending the place of the Rolling Stones in contemporary society.

There was no indication to our parents that either of us was interested in the other. However, later that night I broke up with my boyfriend of three and a half years, and Mehmet spent the next four days trying to reach me through the primitive Bryn Mawr College switchboard. Within a week we were dating, and by the following autumn we were engaged.

Now, I don't think for a minute that you need to have some unexplainable psychic experience to know that the person you are with is right for you. The idea of recognizing your soul mate instantly is very romantic and makes for a cute story to tell the grandkids, but it's far from the litmus test of a good relationship. Many couples take years to ease from a comfortable friendship into the bond of deep marital love. The truth is chemistry, in the purely physical sense, is overrated.

Okay, stop scoffing. Easy for me to say, right? Especially after I just told you this primal attraction story. I feel a bit like one of those annoying supermodels who insists that getting paid to have her hair and makeup done and then smile while a man with a sexy accent takes her picture isn't all it's cracked up to be. It's not that I don't think animal attraction is great. It is! It's just not essential.

Think about it. The vast majority of marital unions throughout the history of mankind didn't originate with two people falling madly in love and *then* getting married. While this was possibly the method of choosing a mate back when we were hunter-gatherers, since we've moved on to agrarian/industrial cultures most couples have been lucky if they have actually gotten to see each other before the wedding day. Even in this century in many parts of the world, marriage is viewed as a financial arrangement, frequently determined by the parents rather than the participants themselves.

Given that reality, I'm convinced there must be something other than physical chemistry that enables a couple to share an outstanding sexual relationship. It's far too important a part of the human experience to be limited to people who are turned on by the mere sight of each other. Truly great sex, the kind that blows your mind and opens your heart, is far more about the soul than the body.

Sex and God

Soul-mate love is both the destination and the journey. In this most simple yet significant act of erotic love, we approach the universal mystery. Here we consciously move from our existential aloneness into a merging with the other. This surrender of ego is, in its absolute form, union with God. Through conscious bonding with another we reflect and manifest collective oneness.

There's an ancient Hermetic principle, "As above, so below." Swedenborg refers to it as the "Law of correspondences." Essentially, what it means is that everything on the material plane is a reflection of, and is connected to, something in the spiritual realm. This is true of rocks and lions and water, and it is especially true of sex. The union of the male and female energies is not merely the origin of human life in the reproductive sense but the very basis of life in the universe.

In Kabbalah the erotic is an image of Shechinah, the divine creative force. This holy sexual energy, while grounded in the physical act of intercourse, is fundamentally spiritual in nature, creating a transcendent joining of souls as well as bodies. Ultimately, as the fullest expression of connectedness, it can become something holy. Sex itself is not truly erotic if it doesn't lead away from the ego. The heart of eros is the drive out of the self toward the other. It's the urge to connect—to give and receive of the true self.

According to Swedenborg, sex is a mirroring of God's relationship with creation and is a representation of the Divine itself. When the masculine and feminine energies come together in sex, they become an image of love being united with truth, which is the essence of God.

Want to know what else Swedenborg said? (This is honestly one of the best parts of being a Swedenborgian.) He claimed that because a man and woman together most closely approximate the Divine, true marital love or what he called "conjugial love" is eternal, and those deep soul bonds remain after death. And this is the good part: couples in heaven still have sex. How cool it that? Of course, if you think about it, why wouldn't you? I mean *sex* is the ultimate form of expressed love, not lounging on a cloud, strumming a harp.

Laws of Attraction

You pick your potential spouse for many reasons. A lot of them have something to do with ensuring the survival of your offspring. Traits like an inclination to protect or nurture, a strong genetic makeup, and the ability to provide food in times of hardship increase the odds that your children will survive to produce children of their own. There are also reasons for choosing a mate that have absolutely nothing to do with procreation. A great smile, a love of bird-watching, and a droll sense of humor could all be essential requirements for your ideal partner.

But even if you are extraordinarily particular about your "type" and your list of necessary attributes is several pages long, on a planet of more than three billion people, I'm sure there are at least a few thousand who would meet your requirements. So what makes you choose one person and not another? Well, according to relationship expert Harville Hendrix, it's not the person's most appealing qualities that seal the deal. It's actually his or her negative traits that attract you. These are not just any old negative traits, like picking one's nose or leaving clothes on the floor, but specifically traits that trigger issues from your past. Over the years you create a psychological imprint of what your collective emotional experience represents. When you find someone who resonates with that image, you're hooked. Hendrix calls this image the imago. (An imago is also a sexually mature insect, but we won't get into that now.)

Hendrix claims that we are subconsciously drawn to people who will provide us with the opportunity to heal our childhood wounds. This is embarrassingly clear in my own life. My dad is a cardiac surgeon. When I was growing up, he was building a career as the youngest-ever chief of cardiothoracic surgery, a member of every major academic society in his field, a highly skilled clinician, and a widely respected researcher. Yeah, I know, sounds familiar. You can just stop it with the Electra jokes right now. The point is that he was very busy—so busy that as a young girl I never felt like I was given enough time. I adored my father and wanted nothing more than to spend every waking moment with him, which was, frankly, impossible. As a five-year-old I naturally assumed that if I were a better daughter, he would want to be with me—that my father's interest in the rest of the world was due to some inadequacy on my part.

Fast forward a few decades and I was still in the same place, much to my dismay—deeply attached to a man who had interests besides bonding with me. And though I understood the situation on a rational level, somewhere deep in my subconscious I was responding as an insecure, rejected little girl.

Now the incredible part is that, while Mehmet meets my imago requirements perfectly, I fulfill his as well. The amazing thing about the way an intimate relationship works is that in it, both partners get what they *need* from the other (which, by the way, is never what you think it will be). Your partner does this partly by *not* always giving you what you want. It is precisely his capacity to make you uncomfortable that creates the challenges that help you grow. This dance of loving each other madly but driving each other nuts provides an opportunity not just to connect with the other but also to learn about yourself—to bring to the surface all those qualities you try to keep hidden, to test yourself beyond anything you could ever imagine. Union with another ultimately takes you inside yourself to a place where all illusions and pretense are stripped away.

Take a minute and examine your own sexual partnership. If you've been together for any length of time, you'll notice that your partner has the ability to press buttons you didn't even know you had. The issues that show up are precisely the ones necessary to teach the lessons you need most.

According to Hendrix, these conflicts with your loved one arise in order to bring up hurt from your past that you can now readdress as a conscious adult with your partner rather than with your parents. When you and your lover work together by carefully listening and agreeing to change for each other, Hendrix believes you can give each other the love you need to heal the wounded child within each of you.

I have a slightly different take. I don't think you can ever get enough love from another person to fill up that chasm of inadequacy that childhood has left in each of us (regardless of how wonderful our parents were). There is nothing your partner can tell you, show you, or give you that will make you whole. You may feel really good while he's stroking you and kissing you and gazing into your eyes, but deep down that doesn't change how you feel about yourself. And that's a good thing. Because it's precisely your partner's inability to give you what you want that forces you to realize that you don't actually need it.

Back to me again, and my recurrent desire to have my husband spend more time focusing just on me. For years I tried to convince him to show his love for me in ways that I believed would help me get over my early years of perceived paternal indifference. It didn't work. First of all, no matter how much he did, it was never enough. My craving for his attention was and is insatiable. The more time we spent together, the more I wanted, so I was setting him up to fail.

Second, being all lovey-dovey Mr. Romantico is not in his nature. (Remember what I said about making people change. Ain't gonna happen. Not unless *they* really, really want to—and sometimes not even then.) But that was the real gift of marrying Mehmet. It was precisely knowing that he loved me deeply but that the love would always be insufficient that stimulated *me* to change.

What I thought I wanted was someone who would be the perfect partner, who would long for us to do everything together, even if it was doing nothing. That's a very pleasant scenario for me. I could easily see myself becoming complacent in my identity as the cherished wife. But that wasn't what my soul needed. Souls know they have to be stretched and pushed and taken to places that may not be so comfortable. What my soul required was autonomy and strength and the refusal to live vicariously through anyone else. Growth for me is not in the direction of being more attached, more committed, and more cuddly. I can do that with my eyes closed and both hands tied behind my back. Independence within a loving relationship is where it all gets scary and dangerous for me, and that's what being married to Mehmet is about.

This may not be your path. Your soul may be seeking out a partner who stimulates more intimacy (which is partly why Mehmet chose me). Maybe you need to be more generous or more forgiving or less demanding. Whatever it is—trust me—it will be uncomfortable. And it will be exactly what you're resisting when you and your loved one hit those areas of discord. Ask yourself where your soul needs to grow. And see how the lover you chose is helping to take you there.

Work It

Some people like to say, "Marriage is no picnic." Actually, I think it sort of is. Certainly eating outside is not the easiest way to ingest a meal. There are ants and bees and the looming possibility of rain. And if you forget something important, like forks and plates, you're screwed. But mostly, a picnic is fun—especially if you can avoid the insects, don't mind getting wet, and enjoy eating with your fingers. Yep, it's a lot like marriage.

Mehmet and I have been married for almost twenty-five years, and while it has been the most rewarding, pleasurable, and joyous time of our lives, it has also been a period of genuine struggle and frustration. When people ask us how we've managed to stay together so long (what is twenty-five in dog years?), I never quite know how to answer. On the one hand we've been very lucky. I am so very grateful for the blessing that our life together has been. We haven't had to face the type of stressors that really try a marriage—things like serious illness, death in the family, and financial crisis. (Knock on a whole lumberyard.) My heart goes out to couples who endure the magnitude of suffering that those situations create. But the normal stuff that comes up in an intimate relationship is plenty to generate all kinds of strife.

So how do you turn that strife into something meaningful and enduring? Truthfully, the answer is different for each couple. I've seen all kinds of relationships that suit those particular partners' needs but in which I would have withered and died. It really depends on what you both want and what you're willing to do to get it. But that being said, there are a few things that I've noticed which seem to be essential in most long-lasting romantic partnerships.

Let me say straight up that marriage is hard work. That's not a bad thing. It's work in the same way as exercise: when you love it, you barely even notice. Still, it takes commitment, creativity, and a willingness to check your ego at the door. Though I'm far from the perfect wife and still have a hell of a lot to learn (besides that twirly thing on a pole), there are a few things I've been attempting in our marriage that I believe can make any partnership better. Hopefully you will see something which you can apply to your own uniquely infuriating, inspiring, uplifting, enlightening, divine gift that is the human sexual bond.

So let's start with the basics. Each one of these is essential for any good relationship. The first is commitment. That's the willingness to stick it out, to say "We're in this together" and actually mean it. It's more difficult than it sounds. The temptation to walk away when things get painful is strong, especially if you enter into a relationship thinking it's supposed to make you feel good all the time. But if commitment isn't something you think you can live up to, forget about marriage and get a pet. You'll save yourself and your would-be spouse a lot of heartache and a hefty lawyer's fee.

The next must-have is honest communication—stress on the word *honest*. This is really two things that when done well fit together seamlessly. The first is effectively articulating your own needs. "Fine," you're thinking, "that's easy." But to really express what you desire, you need to be aware of it. That involves taking a moment to ask yourself what is behind the request. What is it that you're really looking for?

I put on a lot of weight with the birth of our last baby, yet for some reason this had no impact whatsoever on my libido. My poor husband would come home late after long stints of intense pressure in the OR and I would insist on keeping him up until all hours of the night. Occasionally he would protest, claiming sheer exhaustion, in which case I would roll over and fume about what a weakling he was. Sometimes he would indulge my advances, but often this left me feeling as frustrated and unfulfilled as when we had started. I thought I was clearly verbalizing what I wanted (sex), but for some reason I wasn't getting what I needed.

One night, after I had failed at seducing him, I was furiously reviewing my mental list of possible reasons he might be falling asleep—they ranged from his having an affair to his struggling with latent homosexuality—when I snapped, "Are you too tired to put your arm around me?" Hurt and surprised, he responded, "Of course not," and quickly snuggled up behind me, enveloping me in both arms. I was so touched by his genuine tenderness that I started to cry. This was what I wanted. It wasn't sex. It was intimacy and affection. What was confusing to me was that sex usually provided those things. Why wasn't it doing so now?

"Do you still find me attractive?" I gulped between sobs. "Of course I do." He hugged me tighter. I felt a tiny bit better. And then that little voice in my head butted in. "Ah! That's what this is about!" And since I was in no shape to argue, I had to admit that, yes, to a large extent, this insatiable need was not for sex but for affirmation that I was desirable. Sex had become a way of proving that I hadn't been ruined by birthing four children. What *was* being ruined was the sex. In the attempt to alleviate my own insecurities, I had robbed it of its real purpose. It was no longer about connection or sharing or creating; it had become just another tool to boost my ego. Wow. That was a scary thought.

"I'm sorry," I said.

"No, I'm sorry," Mehmet replied.

"I've been very selfish," I protested.

"It's not about you," he insisted. And I was about to jump in with "Yes, of course it is!" Because for me, as we discussed in chapter 2, it really is only about me, but this is where the second factor in communicating needed to kick in. That's the part about consciously listening to what the other person is telling you, and thankfully I was feeling safe enough that I could just shut up and let him speak.

He went on to explain that he was frustrated with his job. He loved operating but was constantly having to deal with repetitive, unsolvable problems concerning both his patients and hospital politics. He felt emotionally drained and, when he got home, had nothing left to give. I tried to really hear what he was saying, to understand his underlying unmet need. I got a sense that he was stagnating, and for Mehmet that was tantamount to death. He was depressed but was keeping his energy level so high during the day that no one noticed.

We talked about what he thought would make him happier at work. Through our conversation it became evident that he wanted a steeper learning curve, more variety in his routine, and the chance to have a bigger impact in the world. The answer? A television show! It just popped out of my mouth without ever having crossed my mind. (I blurt like that on occasion.) And in this case, it was the perfect solution. He would be able to influence millions of people, helping them take control of their own health, but would also be able to stretch beyond his comfort zone and grow personally. How it was going to happen we would have to address later. All of that talking had woken him up . . .

Okay, since we're on the topic of sex, the single most important thing I can say about it is "Have it." If you're a newlywed or, frankly, under thirty, I bet you're thinking I've lost my mind. But for those of you who have been through a couple of cycles of the seven-year-itch and have several kids to prove it, you know exactly what I'm talking about. You're exhausted. There's no time. The baby's in the bed with you. Speaking of which, do you even have birth control? And by the way, did you know Britney's on Letterman tonight? Right. "All day in bed" became "once a day" and is now "once a week, if I have to." I can't tell you how many of my middle-aged friends are experiencing what Mehmet likes to call "a sexual famine."

People age, marriages change, relationships evolve, but whatever stage you find yourself and your partner in, sex matters. It doesn't have to be marathon-long or multiorgasmic; heck, it even doesn't have to be traditional "sex" if you're really, really old or have a medical condition. What it does have to be is a deep and powerful connection between the two of you—body and soul. It needs to be a time you set aside for each other, alone, where you reaffirm that there is nothing on earth more precious than your union. So turn off the TV, move the baby to his crib, and have an espresso shot if you need it to wake up, but make time to make love.

One of the reasons people stop having sex is that it gets boring. Same bat-time, same bat-station, same bat-position. I'm not going to give you a list of Kama Sutra–esque techniques or recommend the best line of "adult" toys, but I will suggest that you mix it up a little. And I don't mean just in the bedroom. If you and your partner have nothing to talk about at dinner, it's unlikely you'll have much to express later that night. If you want a more interesting sex life, start with the life part.

Remember when you were first dating and you couldn't wait to share new experiences or learn new things? Much of the erotic connection is that desire to grow and contribute. When we first met, Mehmet and I played a game where we taught each other vocabulary words. (He chose *pusillanimous*, which I already knew, and I taught him *concupiscence*—so very typical of me.) We wanted to impress each other, to prove we could stimulate each other's minds as well as hormones.

When couples get into a routine, when they take each other for granted, when they no longer make an effort, being together loses a lot of its appeal. One thing that I've observed in couples who have been married for a really long time—like forty, fifty, sixty years—and are still happy is that they've found a way to preserve intimacy and maintain the erotic tension. My own parents, who have been together for almost half a century, are still outrightly flirtatious with each other. They continue to find each other attractive and demonstrate that interest through every word and action. They are never bored.

Tricks of the Trade

I have a propensity to dress down. No one would ever accuse me of being a fashionista. I prefer to wear sweats. Retailers generally eye me suspiciously and suggest the sales rack. But around 6:30 I will almost always put on some blush and mascara and dab a little scented oil on the nape of my neck. Sometimes I will even change the sweatshirt.

My daughter Daphne first noticed me doing this when she was a toddler. "Where are you going?" she asked apprehensively. "Nowhere," I answered. "Then why are you looking pretty?" Busted! I was trying to look pretty. I wanted my husband to desire me, and the shlump look is not what he'd call hot.

Don't get me wrong. Mehmet has seen me at my absolute worst—poison-ivy-faced, midlabor, or in the throes of food poisoning. I can hold my own against any good gargoyle. But I think that part of keeping the spark alive in a marriage is staying attracted to each other, and that generally entails at least trying to stay attractive. Really, this isn't so much about how you look. It has more to do with how you feel—about yourself and your partner.

In the early stages of a romantic relationship most people are fairly good at making themselves desirable. They shower, shave, and use minty-fresh mouthwash. More important, they flirt, which loosely translated means they smile, make eye contact, and laugh at bad jokes. What this adds up to is a loud, clear signal that you think the other person is worth your attention. Make sure that your lover knows you still think he or she is worth it.

One way to ensure your sexual energies stay charged is to be aware of male and female polarity. These are the differences that draw us to each other. It's the magnetism of opposing forces that exists not just in nature but within the very fabric of our psyche. The whole yin/yang, soft/hard, dark/light, feminine/masculine thing is very real when it comes to maintaining attraction. Don't allow yourself to become too androgynous. And don't expect your partner to think like you. (Odds are your lover won't.) The variety in your perceptions and responses is how you complete each other. It's what keeps the chemistry cooking.

Something that absolutely doesn't work in relationships is being too demanding. You may or may not get what you're asking for, but either way you're not winning any brownie points. Rather than complaining and whining, try to be the change you want to see. Whether it's romance or excitement, stop waiting for the other person to initiate. You can create it. Instead of nagging your spouse about spending more time with the kids, go read to them yourself. Rather than harping on the fact that he or she really needs to lose weight, take another lap around the block. Creative energy flows in the direction of focus, so you'll get much better results and generate a positive shift in the relationship if you concentrate on making constructive change in your own life instead of dwelling on the negative traits of your partner.

Finally, learn to fight right. Since dealing with conflict is a big part of any close, long-term relationship, it's essential to know how to air your differences productively. Try to remember what your actual goal is. Too often the whole argument becomes about nothing more than being right. And believe me, being right is overrated—especially when it comes at the price of damaging your most intimate relationship. Your spouse is not your adversary. You don't really want to "beat" your partner, because he or she is on your team. Realize that anything you do or say to hurt your lover will end up hurting you too.

Remember that being mad is no excuse for being unkind. It is horrifying to see how quickly a loving relationship can deteriorate into an all-out verbal brawl, complete with threats, insults, and name-calling. If you find that you tend to behave like this when you get angry, you may want to try turning on a recording device during the argument. Listen to it a few days later, once you've cooled off a bit, and I guarantee you will be both shocked and embarrassed. You can have a disagreement and still treat your partner with civility and respect.

Be up-front with your expectations and requests. Don't assume your lover will be able to read your mind—especially in a fight. And you're probably not going to like this suggestion, but it's generally a good idea to be the first to say you're sorry.

Sometimes it's better just to avoid the fight altogether. Over the course of twenty-five years' worth of arguments, one of the things I realized I had to do was to practice restraint. I needed to let the little things slide and figure out when it was better not to say anything. Basically, I had to manage my own molehills. Constant agitation over small things creates a pervasive feeling of negativity in a relationship and undermines genuine affection.

One of the things I definitely had to let go of was my anger over former girlfriends. I hated the fact that Mehmet had even been "in like" with anyone other than me. The emotion was an incongruous mix of insecurity and contempt, which is a hideous combination. Invariably, I would take my frustration out on him, and of course there was nothing he could do. He couldn't erase his past, no matter how much it bothered me. This was my issue. I needed to deal with it.

Now, I'm not saying you should just suck it up and keep it to yourself when something's bothering you. Repression only works for so long. Eventually rage you hold in will accumulate and explode out of you. You want to attend to issues as they come up, but make sure they are things that actually have a solution that needs to be addressed by the two of you. If you can fix it yourself, do it.

I believe that depth in a relationship comes from sticking it out through the tough times. It's in these moments that the real learning and strongest bonding take place—when we develop as individuals and as a couple. We all experience periods of indifference, betrayal, or disappointment, episodes in our lives when it would be easier just to walk away. But genuine loving relationships are built on commitment to something higher than the individual egos involved.

That said, if you've come to a point where being together is no longer about authentic connection on a higher level, when you or your partner is made less rather than more by the union, then it's time to move on. Forgive yourself and your former lover for any hurt you may have caused each other. Honor the love that you had by refusing to twist it into animosity, and be grateful for the lessons that you learned through your time together. I have to admit I'm really terrible at that part. (I have contracted several hit men to strike Mehmet down if he ever tries to leave me.) But I know that that feeling is not coming from a place of love. True love desires the other's happiness as much as one's own and knows that people are never possessions.

Yeah, I still gotta work on that one. Maybe if we just have more sex . . .

EXERCISE

Holy Sex, Batman!

In this exercise we try to reunite the sacred and the sensual in our own bedrooms. You'll need to find twenty minutes each day for a week when you can lock the door and remain alone, uninterrupted by the phone, children, or curious neighbors. If you don't have a beloved at the moment, that's no excuse not to participate. In this case just meditate naked. Remember, I told you to lock the door.

DAY 1. Tonight (or this morning if you're *those* kinds of people) you're going to play a game. It's sort of like strip poker. Fully dressed, get comfortable on the bed or floor. Take turns finishing this sentence: "I really love it when . . ." It can be something as innocent as "you email me just to tell me you love me" or as provocative as "you bite my nipple." In return for a heartfelt compliment, the other person will remove an article of clothing. When you are both left with only underpants (or a single sock if you went for the good stuff first), then switch the sentence to "I would really love it if . . ." Discard last items of wardrobe and enjoy.

DAY 2. Take off all your clothes and sit facing each other. Allow only the bottoms of your feet to touch. It's the union of souls through the union of soles. (I remember trying this when Mehmet and I were first married and had just read Kurt Vonnegut's *Cat's Cradle*. In that book the technique is called bokumaru.) Stay in this position for at least ten minutes without breaking eye contact and try not to talk too much. When the ten minutes are up, you can do whatever you like.

DAY 3. Tonight is kiss and tell. Get onto the bed naked but without touching each other. Have your partner lie down and close his eyes while you give him a kiss, anywhere you like. I suggest starting with places like the eyelids, lips, or cheek and moving to more erogenous zones as you continue. You get seven kisses. Before each kiss, tell your partner, "This kiss is for the time . . ." and fill in with your own favorite memories. For example, "the time we made love in that abandoned barn," or "the time you brought me flowers after I threw up on your shoes." Just pick an event that you shared for which you are truly grateful. When you get to seven, switch.

DAY 4. Sit on the floor cross-legged, man on the bottom, woman on his lap, facing him with her legs wrapped around his waist. Gaze into each other's eyes and begin breathing together. Take a slow inhalation through the nose for a count of four. Make sure it's a slow, deep, belly breath. Hold for a count of four and then exhale through the nose on four. Now hold for four before you inhale again. Do this together for five minutes. Then start to alternate. As your partner exhales, you inhale. Hold together, then you exhale while he or she inhales. Again hold. Do this cycling breathing for another five minutes.

DAY 5. Lie next to each other naked on the bed. Get as close as you can without actual penetration. Completely relax, and bring your awareness to the very base of your spine. Sense the energy here. Suggest that your lover do the same. Push your pelvis into your partner and feel your energies unite. Slowly focus together on moving that combined energy up your bodies to your lower abdomens. This is your sexual center, so allow the energy to build intensity here. Then continue to move the energy up along past your solar plexus and into your hearts. Again, see it strengthen and expand, converting erotic desire to unconditional love. Make sure your hearts are pressed close. Let your energy flow higher, through your throat, up along your third eye, and then up to the crown of your heads. When it reaches this point, see it radiating out to envelop you both in a radiant white light, which circles back, reinfusing you both with the healing energy of love.

DAY 6. Today focus on being fully present during the act of lovemaking. (That means no wondering if the kids are asleep or fantasizing about Brad Pitt.) As you come together, intently focus on each of your senses. Really look at your partner. Take in the curve of his jaw and the swirl of his chest hair. (If it's a woman, you can ignore the chest hair.) Breathe in his odor and recognize that as his unique scent. Listen to his heartbeat and his gentle moans of pleasure. Taste him. Feel him. Let all your awareness be completely absorbed by the embodiment of your lover. Allow yourself to truly take in who he is, and respond to him in that moment.

DAY 7. Try to bring the erotic into the everyday. Whatever the activity, see if you can relate to it as fundamentally erotic. No, this does not mean looking for phallic shapes in your vegetable soup. What I'm suggesting is that you view every interaction as a play between energetic forces of masculine and feminine energy. When you see your partner throughout the day, focus on your own deep longing to unite with his or her opposing energy. Allow that desire to color everything you do together from eating breakfast to talking on the cell phone while leaving work. See each exchange as an opportunity to express your intense attraction. When you do finally get to the bedroom (or the backseat if you just can't wait any longer), remember that what you are doing is far bigger than this single act. On a cosmic, energetic level it is the very foundation of the universe.

CHAPTER 7

Family

∞

F amilies are the ultimate relationship arena. It's here that we experience our first, deepest, most complex and sometimes most painful interactions. In spite of the inevitable dysfunction that exists in all families, they generate a certain intimacy and honesty that we rarely encounter elsewhere. There is a permanence to families—even broken ones. They remain a part of our lives on a fundamental level regardless of time passed or distance between members.

One of the most noticeable things about our familial relationships is that while the definition stays the same (once a daughter, sister, or mother, we are always that), what that role means in our life changes as we change. We gain or relinquish responsibilities as dependent, caregiver, partner, or even adversary. As we grow from child to adult, spouse to parent, who we are is characterized in large part by our place in the family.

There is a whole network of people who, through blood or marriage, make up our nearest and dearest. Parents, siblings, in-laws, aunts, uncles, and cousins—the whole family tree plays a crucial role in our development. This is clearly evident in our younger years. But even as we become more independent and start new families of our own, those early connections are still some of the most important.

The seminal relationships for each of us are with our parents. In many ways they set the tone for all subsequent relationships. Hundreds of miles and decades of therapy will probably still not fully erase the imprint of those formative bonds. How we approach our friends, lovers, teachers, employers, and children is colored by those first human interactions. Even the way we envision God is influenced by whether we saw our parents as kind and caring or authoritarian and retributive.

My own parents could not have been better. They were loving, supportive, patient, engaged. They raised me in a way that was pretty close to perfect. Nevertheless, I'm rife with all sorts of issues. Bizarrely, even good parenting can leave scars.

The thing to keep in mind as you mature and attempt to approach your life with more awareness is that no matter what your parents were like, you are now an adult and are responsible for your own choices. You *can* behave differently from the way you were conditioned to. You don't have to react to situations based on how you felt as a four-year-old. It's not easy, but it's also not impossible.

Start with gratitude and forgiveness. Thank your parents for everything they gave you—including your very existence. Then release the pain of their mistakes by forgiving them for where they fell short and for the ways they may still be imperfect. Try to reestablish your relationship with them based on who they are now, not the people you perceived them to be thirty years ago. Sometimes your parents will resist the shift from an adult/child relationship to a more peer-based one. Just remember to be respectful; they're still your parents regardless of how old you are.

Siblings provide another wonderful opportunity for working on conscious relationship. You have different tastes, opinions, desires, needs, yet you are closer biologically and often emotionally to them than to anyone else on the planet. Plus, you're stuck with them. You can't divorce your blood. You can never *not* be a sister or brother the way you can stop being someone's friend.

I've been blessed with extraordinary siblings, but as close as we are, we still have areas of conflict and opportunities to behave as mature adults or to revert to old childhood patterns. As the eldest of six, I grew up assuming the role of ringleader and surrogate mother. "Bossy" would be a very kind way of describing my demeanor. I was the big kid: I knew better so I decided what everybody would do. This was fine when I was ten and my little sister was three. It doesn't work so well now that we're middle-aged women.

It's very difficult for me to remember that my siblings are perfectly capable of making their own decisions. But respecting each other's choices is one of the key elements of living in a healthy relationship. I learned this the hard way years ago when one of my sisters decided to date a troll. Okay, he wasn't *really* a troll, but he was pretty close. I was convinced he was a dreadful choice and made it my business to point out this fact every time we were together.

My efforts failed miserably. Instead of thanking me for my insights on her creepy boyfriend, my sister just stopped hanging out with me. (The nerve!) In my attempt to manage her life, I had lost the trust, intimacy, and respect that had always defined our relationship. Some time later she saw his evil troll horns too and broke up with him, but she had also seen something rather unpleasant in me, and it was a long while before we were able to rebuild the kind of bond we had once had.

I think part of the problem is that on some deep level we believe that our family is an extension of ourselves, so their choices and behavior reflect on us. If they do something that we don't approve of, our very identity is threatened. There's a primal pack mentality within a shared gene pool that says, "We are one. Your survival is my survival; your failure is also mine." When they disappoint or embarrass us, we sometimes push them away to prove that we are not the same. But mostly we just try to control them.

In-laws are another area of complicated family dynamic. They're sort of like the surprise-free gift that comes in a box of Cracker Jacks. All you really wanted was the caramel popcorn, but now you've got the superspy secret decoding ring that pinches your finger when you put it on. It's extra tricky because you are in a situation of close proximity but without the blood bond that you have with your own kin. No matter how delightful they may be, you will have some areas of discord. It's one of those universal guarantees.

My in-laws are pleasant-enough people. They are friendly, intelligent, and charming, yet whenever we are together for an extended period of time, say, more than ten minutes, everyone becomes very uncomfortable. Fundamentally, they are a traditional Middle Eastern family and I am an outspoken, hot-blooded American woman. Much to their ongoing chagrin I am devoid of most of the feminine attributes they admire—docility, reticence, and complacency. While they appreciate that I love their son, they have always felt that a different type of woman would be a better companion— someone more like a blow-up doll.

Our issues are not necessarily personal, but it would be a cop-out to say they're strictly cultural. Problems arise between us because we have values based on our individual biases and these are inherently in conflict. In the outside world we would probably deal with our differences by choosing not to associate with each other. This is not always an option in families. And (I can say this after years of struggle) this is a *good* thing. A difficult relationship is in many ways the same as any other relationship. It still requires the ongoing attempt at self-observation, compassion, and nonattachment.

The greatest lesson I learned from living in relationship with my in-laws was that if I had a problem with them, then to some extent I *was* the problem. Which is a beautiful thing, because as I've mentioned before, the only person I can change is myself.

Specifically, I had to change my expectations. For a long time I had been attached to the idea that they ought to act in a particular way (which in retrospect seems pretty foolish). To some extent we all believe that other people should do what *we* would do in any given situation. But living with this assumption only sets us up for disappointment. When I gave up judging my in-laws by my personal criteria of what was and wasn't acceptable and focused instead on my reaction to them, our relationship improved significantly.

All of our differences aside, I am permanently in their debt for raising the man I love. I am married to their son and they come with the package. But they are only as much a part of my emotional life as I allow them to be. If there's drama, it's because I'm permitting myself to get sucked in. I realize living with any family can be challenging, but when approached consciously, with a sincere attempt at self-reflection and a dedication to honesty, the experience can be one of the greatest catalysts for personal growth.

Baby Steps

My kids challenge me, mold me, in many ways define me. The relationship, at least in terms of influence, is definitely a two-way street. Being a mother is the most rewarding and the most frustrating thing I have ever done. But for right now, it's what I do. It's who I am.

We've all heard—and it's absolutely true—that when you have a child you become hostage to fortune; you feel like your heart is walking around outside your body. If you're a parent, you know that these sayings don't come close to half of it. Having a baby is the most terrifying thing you will ever do. (And I'm not referring to labor here. That's barely a blip of discomfort compared to what comes after.) Nothing—and I really mean nothing—makes you more vulnerable than having a child. But it will also bring you inestimable joy and fulfillment.

Scarily, just because you *can* have a baby doesn't mean you have any clue about what to do with her (or him) once she's born. We're not like other mammals with the ability to nurture coded somewhere into the DNA. I remember when I had Daphne and they handed her to me in the delivery room. All I could think was "She's so small. What if I drop her?" Admittedly, I was exhausted after twenty-seven hours of labor and my brain was functioning at a subprimate level, but the truth was that I was completely unprepared to care for an infant.

Thank goodness we were living close to my parents and I went straight to their house from the hospital. My mother was invaluable at that time. She always is, but what she did for those first few weeks after I gave birth was amazing. She took care of me so that I could take care of Daphne. There was something profound and archetypal about the female bond between generations.

It was a unique time in my life—definitely in that liminal space we talked about earlier. I was on the threshold between being a child and becoming a mother. I experienced not just the birth of my daughter but the rebirth of myself—of my identity as a woman rather than a girl.

I'm not for a second suggesting that you are less than fully a woman until you've given birth. But I really wasn't. I was twenty-two at the time, without clear direction or a sense of responsibility.

All that changed after Daphne. Having a baby makes you grow up quickly. You are no longer free to pursue whatever you want—even if all you want is to sleep through the night.

We are biologically programmed to connect with our babies. The hormones surging through our bodies make us love them no matter what. That doesn't mean this love is straightforward or uncomplicated. Postpartum depression is real and very serious for many women. But even for those of us who have never had a mood swing, there are a million minor things that interfere with our ability to bond with our child. Everything from outside time demands to self-generated obstacles like impatience and insecurity conspire to rob us of that unique experience that is the mother/infant relationship.

My only advice is to cherish this time. It passes so fast. Bring your personal work on living with conscious presence to the moments you get to share with your infant. Breathe her in, hold her close, gaze into her beautiful eyes. While you obviously have other things in your life that will need attention, when you are alone with your baby, let yourself really be there. Focus completely on the unique relationship that the two of you share.

As an infant, your child is pretty much perfect. Babies burp, poop, or cry and you act like they've just won a Nobel prize. If they smile, it's heaven on earth. But once they turn into toddlers, everything changes. They start to develop into individuals with their own desires and aversions. They defy you, ignore you, and use *no* in every other sentence. When they start to assert their own little wills, then the real dance of parenthood begins. You need to remember that you're the grown-up and not take it personally when your child resists total submission. If you let your ego be threatened by your child's ego, then any attempt at conscious interaction is forfeit.

On the other hand, reluctance to be an authority figure is an equally dangerous parenting pitfall that I've seen myself and many of my friends succumb to. We love our children so much that we want them to be happy—and that's a good thing—but too often we equate being happy with having every single demand met instantaneously, which is not good. It's really important for toddlers to understand that they don't rule the house. Getting everything all the time does not make them happy. It makes them little tyrants. Toddlers need to learn to process disappointment and respond appropriately. Life is going to show them that they don't always get what they want. Far better that lesson come early and in a compassionate way from a loving parent.

When Daphne was around two years old, she ruled the roost. She was (and is) extremely bright and adorably cute, which enabled her to manipulate her father and me more thoroughly. I remember one night when Mehmet was on call. I had gone to Philadelphia for the evening and was supposed to attend an event where children were not invited. After much deliberation I finally consented to leave her with a trusted family member for a few hours. Being the Six that I am, I worried through the entire cocktail portion of the evening, barely able to toss down a few tasteless mini spanakopitas and a glass of chardonnay. When the salad was served, I called home, just to check that everything was all right. Big mistake. Daphne got on the phone, and as soon as she heard my voice, she began to wail. I was in the car driving to pick her up before the main course arrived at the table.

This was not about wanting Daphne to be happy. This was about allowing my own apprehension to be transferred to my daughter. When I called, it was for my own peace of mind, not hers. Daphne sensed this fear and assumed it as her own. Rather than encouraging confidence, independence, and resilience, I actually increased her separation anxiety by behaving in a way that implied that something was wrong if we were apart.

Kids need to feel safe and protected, but they also need to learn to experience the world by taking risks. They grow through the success or failure of *their* efforts, not ours. If we micromanage our children's lives, we send a message that they are incompetent on their own. When they don't face challenges because we shelter them from any discomfort or emotional stress, they are unable to discover their true capabilities and claim their inner strength.

Hot Mama

After the birth of my third daughter, Zoe, I was feeling particularly mommified—which, for those of you who haven't been there, is not entirely unlike being mummified. There is that same sense of claustrophobia and accumulation of dust, the vague recognition that life as you knew it is over, and the sneaking suspicion that your brain has been sucked out through your nose. The major difference is that you don't have the gauzy bandages holding everything in place, which means it all bulges.

I had just turned thirty-one but I felt closer to fifty. I was exhausted, sagging, and stretched. I felt about as sexy as a Jell-O mold. And *sexy* is my favorite adjective. So, when Zoe reached the ripe age of six weeks, I decided I needed to do something drastic. I wasn't quite sure what it was going to be, but it had to be something decidedly unmommyish. I needed to reclaim the part of me that had actually gotten pregnant in the first (and second and third) place. I wanted my sexy back.

Now, if I were rational or disciplined or just had any common sense, the obvious thing to do would have been to hit the gym. But truthfully, this wasn't so much about the way I looked as the way I felt about myself. I needed to shift what was in my head more than what was in my mirror. I was disgusted by what I thought I had become—dowdy, dull, drab. I wanted to be wild and exciting and spontaneous and unpredictable. I fantasized about jumping out of planes or becoming a NASCAR driver. But neither was really feasible while breast-feeding.

And then a miracle occurred. No seas parting or bushes burning, just one of those perfect moments of synchronicity that happen all the time but only reveal their miraculousness much later. I was taking the baby for a stroll with my friend Jen. We were in a neighborhood we had never visited before, and we turned down a side street and were about halfway down the block when we passed a tattoo parlor. Tattoo parlors by their very nature tend to be a bit seedy, but this one took seedy to a whole new level. Skulls, daggers, barbed wire, and blood were the happy themes that permeated the window display.

"God." Jen rolled her eyes as we walked by.

I know it's used as an expression, but when someone says "God," I think of God, and while I was thinking of God, I had this very weird impulse to go inside the tattoo joint.

"Want to get a tattoo?" I asked Jen.

"Yeah, right." She laughed.

I stopped walking. "How about just getting our belly buttons pierced?"

"Are you out of your mind?" she retorted with derision.

"I'm serious."

She looked around to see if she could catch a glimpse of the aliens who had abducted the real Lisa and substituted an insane version.

"Come on," I insisted.

As I wheeled the stroller through the door, I began to have second thoughts. On the wall closest to me was a poster advertising a Wiccan black Sabbath and the boy behind the counter had more metal in his face than I have in my garage.

"Can I help you?" he mumbled, his tongue encumbered by the barbell at its tip.

"Nope. We're just looking," Jen responded almost before he had asked.

"Let's go—now," she whispered as she pulled the stroller away from me.

"I'd like to get my belly button pierced," I declared, probably way too loud, because they both looked at me like I was a bit off.

"Do you have anything in gold?" I added, much more quietly.

The boy smirked. Jen groaned. And ten minutes later I had a ring in my navel.

So, what was the miracle? Was I suddenly transformed into the sex kitten I longed to be? Well, no. But ironically I did instantly become a better parent. In that single act I became Lisa again. Not Mrs. Oz. Not Mom. Just me. Doing something for myself that had nothing to do with nurturing another being melted away a lot of the frustration and resentment that I had been carrying without even knowing it.

I find that with many of us mothers, in our effort to take care of everyone around us we end up neglecting ourselves. And I don't just mean physically. We talked about that a little in chapter 4, but along with forgetting to take our own vitamins often comes skipping showers, eschewing sleep, and reading nothing but the backs of cereal boxes.

The stressed, unfulfilled, overworked parent is a less than optimal parent. Making time for yourself is not about narcissism. It's a means of recharging and refocusing so you can reconnect with your family. A woman who has no sense of who she is other than "mother" risks becoming bitter when one day the kids have grown and left the house, taking her identity with them.

I can't emphasize enough how important it is to have your own thing. Virginia Woolf entitled her most notable feminist essay "A Room of One's Own." I don't care if you have a whole room. It can be a corner, a closet, a drawer if that's all you can spare, but it's crucial that you permit yourself to have a modicum of independence from your duties as wife, mother, daughter. Beneath the nursing bra and dishwater hands is the girl who won the regional lacrosse championship or edited her college newspaper.

Indulge a passion. Express your inner creativity. Learn a new skill that will stimulate your body and/or mind. Do anything that reminds you that you have value to the world as something more than a broodmare. Then, when you go back to the kids, you will have much more to share with them—even if it's just the knowledge that rings are probably better on fingers.

Walk the Talk

As the kids get bigger, our relationship with them evolves. We are no longer the source of all things—perfection embodied in the form of the universal mother. They start to develop discernment and evaluate our behavior as a gauge for their own. At this point it's imperative that, if you want to influence your children, you strive to practice what you preach. They pick up your values even when you don't think you're broadcasting them, so be aware of what you're teaching with your actions.

Years ago, when our daughter Arabella was in eighth grade, we had the opportunity to take the kids on a business trip to New Mexico. Mehmet had to attend one meeting, but the rest of the time we could ski and visit a Navaho reservation. It was over the Presidents' Day weekend, but we had to leave on Friday morning, so the older girls would miss a day of school. This wouldn't normally be a problem, but their school has a policy of failing the student for any assignment due during an unexcused absence, and Arabella had a test scheduled for that day.

"Mommy, I can't come skiing," she sobbed when she got home

one afternoon about a week before our trip. "My adviser said no."

I was ticked. I picked up the phone and called him immediately. He answered politely and, when I questioned him on his decision with Arabella, referred me to the section on absences in the school handbook. He correctly assumed that I didn't have the volume open in front of me, so he began reading out loud in that annoyingly insipid administrator voice.

"Yes, I know the rule," I interrupted, unable to take the droning a moment longer. "I'm asking you to excuse her for that day."

"Extending a family vacation is not a valid reason for an excuse." Why he was still using the automaton voice was a mystery to me.

"And what is?" I snapped.

"Extenuating circumstances such as illness, emergencies, death . . ." He was reading from the handbook again.

"How about extenuating circumstances like nonrefundable tickets?"

There was a pause and then he said, very matter-of-factly, "I think illness is your only option."

"Illness?" I was so shocked by the disappearance of Mr. Roboto that I couldn't quite process what he was suggesting.

"Call the school the morning of the day she is going to miss and report that she is sick."

"Fine. How about I tell you right now. On next Friday Arabella is going to have a sore throat."

I had barely said the words when I caught Arabella's eye. I had been so wrapped up in the conversation that I had forgotten she was with me. Her expression was a combination of surprise, confusion, and disappointment. I was lying to her school right in front of her. The irony was that she had recently been punished for telling us she would be at a friend's house when she was actually somewhere else. She wanted to come on the trip, but not like this. Not if it meant sacrificing her mother's integrity.

Now, you may be thinking, "What's the big deal? A small white lie never hurt anyone." And you could be right. But not in our family. With the kids we've always made it clear that we can handle almost any type of bad behavior, but if they lie about it, that's another thing altogether. Then it's "grounded for life." Many of the qualities we desire for ourselves and our children—integrity, honor, courage—are embodied in the simple act of stating the truth. And there is almost nothing more damaging to relationships than the inability to trust because of dishonesty in one or both parties.

I have made a point (over my husband's objections) of raising our children without a tooth fairy, without an Easter bunny, and without Santa Claus because I didn't want them to get big, learn the truth, and look at me the way my daughter was looking at me at that moment. In that three-minute phone call I was thoughtlessly undermining her entire moral upbringing. I felt sick.

"Actually, she's going to be perfectly healthy," I quickly corrected. "And she will be on a plane to Albuquerque."

"But I just told you the only way she would be excused—"

"Yes, I know. Thank you." I quickly hung up before he could respond.

Arabella came over and gave me a hug. "I'm going to fail my test."

"Probably," I responded, hugging her tighter and knowing that she had just helped me pass mine.

Growing Pains

Remember I said you can't change anyone else? Well, that's not entirely true when it comes to your children. Parents have a remarkable amount of influence over the behavior of their offspring, both good and bad; they don't control them completely . . . and certainly not predictably. I know couples who were absolute monsters but whose children grew up to be kind, responsible, emotionally stable adults. I also know people who were conscientious, caring, involved parents whose kids ended up in jail or rehab. There's always some unforeseen and uncontrollable factor that impacts your child's development—including forces within them. However, while acknowledging that they are ultimately responsible for their own choices, there are a few things Mehmet and I try to keep in mind to help guide our kids. I'd love to share them with you.

First, remember to be the parent and don't be afraid to be unpopular. Your job is to help your children grow as strong, moral, compassionate individuals, not to be their best friend. I don't think you need to be super strict, but set your expectations for your children based on your values and insist on behavior that is congruent with them. Try to avoid saying no reflexively, but when you say it, mean it.

My kids are incessantly whining because I won't let them do whatever the rest of their class is doing. From going to R-rated movies to staying out until midnight, if their friends are allowed to do it, they think they should be too. I must admit that it's a lot easier to cave and let them do what they want, especially once the begging begins, but that wouldn't be the right choice.

While your children may say they want more permissive, laissez-faire child rearing, in reality they need someone to set boundaries and provide a predictable structure. Appropriate and consistent discipline creates a sense of security that doesn't exist when there are no consequences. Also, when you don't impose any limits for your child, the implication is that you don't care or that you're just too lazy to do anything about it.

I know there's an ongoing debate over whether the quality or quantity of time with a child is more important. Ideally you'd have both. But since many of us need to work, the quality becomes extra important. This doesn't mean every play date needs to be an event. It's more important that you really commit to being present when you interact. So when you're together, turn off the TV or radio and put down the PDA and magazines. You can do other things, but they should be activities where you can look your child in the eye and have a meaningful conversation.

When Daphne was little, we lived in an apartment with a separate laundry room. Twice a week the two of us would pile several baskets full of sheets, footie pajamas, and hospital scrubs on top of her stroller and schlep down to the basement. It could have seemed like an onerous chore, but it was actually fun because the whole event became a game. She would put in the coins, pour the detergent, and stack the folded clothes. I covered everything else. Doing a necessary task together gave Daphne a sense of contribution and pride and allowed me to spend time with her I may not have otherwise had.

While mutual productivity is great, it's also important to spend some serious do-nothing time with your children. Teenagers especially tend to respond like wild animals. They need to sense they can trust you before they open up. Just hanging out with no agenda shows kids that you value their company and that you enjoy being with them, and that goes a long way in the trust department.

One thing you can be sure of, in your journey as a parent you are going to mess up and make mistakes. And so will your kids. Try not to make too big a deal over it either way. Remember that parenting is a process. It's far more about connection than progress and results.

When you're the one who's lost your temper or let your child down, make sure you say you're sorry—and really mean it. When your kids do stupid things, remember to separate the action from the actor. Don't ever condone bad behavior, but keep your love for your child unconditional. When they are at their worst, they need your love the most. Try to focus on positive behavior rather than dwelling on what they've done wrong. Whether it's toilet training or maintaining a curfew, the natural tendency is to emphasize when mistakes occur. All this does is draw attention to the behavior you want to discourage, ultimately making it more likely to occur. I'm not saying you should ignore it when your child kicks the dog or throws his food on the floor. But once you've addressed it appropriately, move on and get back to noticing all the wonderful things he does.

Most important, show your children that you love them. With every word and every gesture, make sure they know that they are the most valuable things in the world. Because they really are.

EXERCISE
All Together Now

This week is about building family unity. Each day or night you are going to reserve a block of time to connect with those people who mean the most to you.

DAY 1. Have family breakfast together. If you or your spouse normally leaves before everyone else, let your boss know you will be running a little late. Sit down at the table, and before you eat, take a moment to express gratitude that you are a family.

DAY 2. Have family date night. Do something fun all together. Go to dinner or bowling or miniature golf. Or just stay home and play board games. Try to avoid things like movies or

TV. This activity is about bonding, and when you are watching something, you can't really speak to each other.

DAY 3. Make a family values document. Get together for half an hour and brainstorm a list of the things that are important to you and your loved ones. For our family these things are telling the truth, saying you're sorry, letting go of resentment, being considerate of other people's feelings, and sharing whatever you have. Make sure that yours are personally meaningful for each member of your family, then have everyone sign it as a covenant that you will all strive to live by.

DAY 4. Take an evening to revisit old family memories. Watch home videos of when the kids were little or peruse photo albums. Have the children talk about their favorite birthdays or vacations and tell them stories of when you were little.

DAY 5. Have the kids write down what they will be like as parents. If they're too little to write, let them dictate to you. Encourage them to list the ways they will be similar to you in discipline style and how they will be different. You'll probably get lots of "I'll let my kids stay up as late as they want and watch TV all day," but there may also be some "I won't yell at them when they forget to pick up their toys." Look for things you could change in your own parenting approach based on your child's perceptions.

DAY 6. Schedule a date for an extended family party or picnic. Invite as many uncles, great-aunts, and cousins as you can remember. Have everybody bring a dish (with a printout of the recipe) and volunteer to assemble, photocopy, and disseminate your family's personal heirloom cookbook. Also, bring a stack of poster board and markers and have everyone contribute to filling in the family tree.

DAY 7. Make a decision to do something as a group that will benefit people beyond your immediate family. You can volunteer your time at charities like local soup kitchens (I have found a few in New York that allow older children to participate) or make something together that you can donate at a school fundraiser. My kids really enjoy taking flowers to the nearby retirement home and spending time with the residents. You can also set aside some money each month and determine as a family where you will give it. We let each child have a set amount specifically allocated to their own favorite foundations. For example, with the Oz kids, Oliver tends to prefer organizations that seek to preserve the environment or support the troops overseas, while Arabella wants to help orphans. Discover what matters to your family and get involved.

CHAPTER 8

You and Everybody Else

In this chapter I'd like to examine our relationship with humanity as a whole and see how that pertains to our individual personal growth. I want to explore what it means to be a member of the global community—to look at our responsibilities to those close to us and to those simply sharing the planet, because at the most fundamental level we are all connected.

I know that sounds a little fruity. I'm actually reminding myself a tiny bit of an friend of mine who used say things like *"Alone is all one*—when you add *L*, which is *love."* (This is the same woman who suggested I drink my own urine as part of a cleansing fast.) So to counter the wacky factor I'd like to point out that this concept of underlying unity is actually a complex theory of advanced physics.

In 1982 a team of scientists lead by Alain Aspect discovered that subatomic particles were able to communicate instantaneously even when separated by large distances. This posed a bit of a problem because it meant that the information was traveling faster than the speed of light, which according to Einstein should be impossible. The interaction indicated a nonlocal causality, pretty much ruling out space and time as factors in the particles' relationship.

David Bohm, another brilliant physicist, addressed this conundrum by suggesting that the particles behaved in this way because they were not in actuality distinct entities but were part of the same greater whole at a deeper level of reality. Their separateness was mere illusion. He went further to postulate that this union at the quantum level was symptomatic of the interrelatedness of all things. Bohm theorized that the universe could be envisioned as a hologram in which the entirety of creation was contained in each particular, every moment of space and time in all others.

Okay, so the invisible link between subatomic particles may seem a little off the relationship track, I bring it up merely to point out that the idea of a oneness of all things is not just some New Age, patchouli-induced musing. We may not understand how it occurs, but we are connected to everything and are in relationship with all other living beings.

I admit there are times when our interrelatedness seems freakishly weird and anything but scientific. Though our usual paradigm of reality is one of separation and discrete degrees of differentiation, all of us experience unexplainable moments of obvious connection. Instances of ESP, déjà vu, and improbable coincidence make us stop and wonder what's really going on. There's no logical reason that you should know that someone's going to call just before the phone rings or that you should happen to be in the exact right place at the right time to meet the single person who could change your life (as I did the night I met Mehmet). So many things happen that make absolutely no sense if we believe that we exist independently of each other.

Several months ago I had an appointment in the city for which I was running extremely late. I was stuck in unremitting traffic on the West Side Highway and decided to pull off and try my luck with one of the avenues. My luck appeared to be on hiatus, as the street I turned down was under construction, and I ended up having to drive around in a giant circle. Something other than luck was at work that afternoon.

I am utterly enchanted by the wondrous occurrence of synchronicity and witness it in my own life over and over again. That day was one of countless times that I've been somewhere by sheer chance and have seen in retrospect that I was absolutely supposed to be there.

As I pulled up to the light, grumbling to myself that I was going to have to get back on the highway and had just wasted another ten minutes, I noticed a very old homeless man sifting through a trash bin on the corner. There was nothing remarkable about him initially. In New York you come across homeless people every day. But the way he looked at me was startling.

When my eyes met his, it was as if I were transported to another place, where he and I knew each other. He was not a ragged old man, and I was not a New Jersey housewife. We were . . . friends? I know it sounds crazy, but that's the only way I can describe the connection. In my head I heard him say, "I knew you'd come." And I said, "Me too." But I didn't actually say anything because I was still frozen at the light, staring at his face.

I had just been to the bank, which was part of the reason I was late in the first place, so I had a bunch of cash. I looked away just long enough to grab some and roll down the window. He shuffled over and reached toward me. I gave him the money, and as he took it our hands touched. He felt warm and familiar. He smiled, but it wasn't a "thank you" smile or even a "gee, I'll be able to eat to-night" smile. It was more like a smile of benediction.

Then he stepped back and the whole thing dissolved. He was just another homeless man and I was late. I glanced up at the light. It had been through an entire cycle and was turning yellow again. I looked back at "my friend," but he had forgotten me and was head-ing for another garbage can. I hit the gas and gunned it into the in-tersection as the light turned red.

A few minutes later I was back on the highway and—strangely—there was *no traffic*! It had completely cleared in the time I had gone around a few blocks. I zipped downtown and made it to my ap-pointment with several minutes to spare. I have no idea what hap-pened that day, but I did have a glimpse of that deeper level of reality that Bohm postulated—where we are all connected. Where we are all one.

Sphere of Influence

Perhaps these insights don't inspire you to hold hands in a circle and sing "Kumbaya" or "We Are the World" just yet, but I hope that you are giving some thought to the possibility of living in uni-versal relationship. It's important because inherent in that relation-ship is the ability to influence. Each one of us has an impact, either positive or negative—on the people around us, on the human col-lective, and on the planet itself. It may be small—and much of it's invisible in the present moment—but that doesn't mean it's insig-nificant.

You've most probably heard of the "butterfly effect," which re-fers to what scientists call "sensitive dependence on initial condi-tions." This is the idea that ostensibly negligible differences at the start of a calculation can result in a dramatic divergence of the results. It was first demonstrated in the early 1960s by a meteorologist who rounded off his inputs to the nearest thousandth instead of entering the full six digits after the decimal point. Logically, a discrepancy that small shouldn't have made much of a difference. (It was the equivalent of a flap of that butterfly's wing.) But the actual effect of that tiny variance was enormous.

The same principle of seemingly trivial actions causing unimaginably huge shifts is evident in our own lives. You know I believe that you can't actually *make* other people change, but I do think you can initiate or inspire change in those around you, and vice versa. If you look back over your life experiences, I'm sure you can find something someone said or did that altered everything that followed. Maybe it was a teacher who believed in your potential and inspired you to make the most of yourself. Or perhaps you had a lover who allowed you to feel beautiful for the first time. It could also have been something damaging, like a hurtful taunt from other kids on the playground that convinced you to stop playing sports forever.

When I was growing up, one of by best friends was the kind of guy your parents always warn you about. His name wasn't Rocco, but it could have been and I'm going to call him that for the rest of this story. He was reckless and dangerous and terribly charming. He did bad things and made you want to do them too. Drugs, alcohol, and vandalism were his calling cards. At nineteen he was on the fast track to nowhere.

My parents loved him and watched with sadness as he continued to make poor choices. One afternoon, following some debacle in which he had "borrowed" our car at one a.m. to get beer in Jersey, my father sat him down.

"What are you doing with your life?" he asked, genuinely concerned.

"I'm thinking about becoming a roadie," Rocco responded, laughing.

"Have you applied for that job?" Dad was humoring him.

"No. I'm really not sure if I want to do that or be a DJ."

My father's not big on wasting time, so he got right to the point. "There's a course that will train you to work the heart pump in the operating room. If you graduate, I'll hire you. It's a six-figure salary. Think about it." And that was the end of the discussion.

One night. One conversation. It shouldn't have been that big a deal. And truthfully, Rocco didn't seem all that interested. But something changed in their relationship. It could have been the allure of good money or the fact that he had no idea what a roadie actually did, but Rocco embarked on a new path after that. He did eventually take my father up on his offer and worked with him for the next fifteen years. And though he's still outrageous, he doesn't have that self-destructive quality that defined his youth.

The reason I think my father's intervention made a difference was that it altered the way Rocco saw his place in the world. Someone outside his family actually cared about him and his future, and that shifted the way he felt about himself. This change in self-perception altered his life path. Which of course influenced everyone he came in contact with from that point on. Because that's the way the butterfly effect works.

The really cool and absolutely terrifying thing about becoming aware of the impact of your behavior is that you never know for sure what the far-reaching effects will be. Everything you do ripples outward over time, from person to person. You can be cruel or kind; either way, the energy almost never stops with the object of your action but is passed on over and over. Not to add any pressure, but it does make you think twice before doing something that will spread negativity indefinitely. Far better to let your love radiate out into the world.

The Neighbor

I can talk all day about loving everyone on the planet, but putting it into practice is a bit more difficult for me. I'm not by nature what you'd call a "people person." I'm social because I have to be, not because I like it. If given the choice I would always rather stay home with my kids than be out "meeting and greeting." I love a good book, a good movie, a good glass of wine—heck, I'll take a mediocre wine—but don't make me drink it with a room full of other people.

So you can see the inherent conflict. I know intellectually that I exist in relationship with everyone, that my purpose for being is to evolve through service within those relationships, yet it is a great effort for me to embrace this truth in my daily life. And now we're back at that whole wounded-healer-writing-the-self-help-book thing. The sad fact is I'm actually terribly uncomfortable in all but my closest relationships.

Some of you may be born extroverts who get all tingly at the idea of going to a party on Friday night. But for those of you who get cold sweats instead, I'll let you in on a little tip my mother told me that gets me through the worst of my hermitish episodes. She said, "You don't need to like everyone, you just need to love them."

Which was great and made perfect sense in my head, but how exactly do you go about loving everyone? Just saying that you love them is meaningless. Equally pointless is attempting to generate some warm, fuzzy feeling that you loosely associate with the faceless masses. I believe the answer lies in Christ's teaching "Love your neighbor as yourself."

By using the term "neighbor," he wasn't simply referring to people living on the same block or even in the same voting district. (Not that any of the disciples actually had voting rights.) In fact, when he illustrated his concept of neighborly love with the parable of the Good Samaritan, he deliberately picked someone from a different area altogether. He was emphasizing that "the neighbor" is not determined by geographic, cultural, or even personal boundaries. It is defined by something internal. You may think this is an obvious concept, but at the time it was really quite radical, and even today most of us seem to either be ignorant of the fact or choose to forget it. Our tendency is to be deeply attached to the individuals in our immediate circle and not give much thought to anyone else.

Nationality, ethnicity, religion, and political perspective allow us to form lines around sets and subsets of people, whom we then label as similar or different to varying degrees. The ones with whom we identify most closely are the ones we spend our time, emotion, and resources on. But living a life in loving relationship is about more than just taking care of "your own."

Imagine if the heart said, "I'm pumping blood to myself really well, but I can let the rest of the body fend for itself. Those toes are the foot's problem, not mine." We are part of an interconnected system very similar to the body. Just like individual cells aggregated into organs and systems, we have an individual and societal identity, but our ultimate responsibility is to the welfare of the whole. Each of us has a unique function in the greater collective.

Since we're all part of the whole, who then is the "neighbor" that we're supposed to love? If it's all people randomly and indiscriminately, why wouldn't Jesus have just said, "Love everybody"? According to Swedenborg, the neighbor is that inner core of goodness or the "true self." When we love "the neighbor," we seek to serve this interior Divine spark within each person, rather than everybody's individual or collective egos. For example, it would not be "loving your neighbor" if you were helping him be dishonest or harmful or unkind. That's not honoring his higher self. Nor is it acting in a way that's congruent with your own inner core of light and spirit. Our obligation is to encourage and support this best part in others by acting from that same part inside ourselves. We are then loving the neighbor as our self.

The one danger of this approach is that it can be used as an excuse to judge rather than to serve. The way to love is to examine our own actions and make sure that they are fostering only good in the other person, not to determine whether or not that person is worthy of our help.

This issue comes up frequently in conversations about giving money to beggars. I know a lot of people would say, "Don't do it. They'll just go out and buy drugs with it." This may be true. In which case I have to think, "Am I actually serving his (or her) higher being by enabling him to buy drugs?" But then of course I need to follow that question with another, which is "Am I serving his higher self by rejecting him? Does my walking past, not making eye contact, imagining myself to be superior with absolutely no knowledge of his past, inspire him to realize the error of his ways and throw away that crack pipe once and for all?" Hardly.

Also, if he is a drug addict (which is by no means evidenced by the mere fact that he needs money), then what kind of pain must he be in? How can I, in my safe, privileged position, judge him for wanting to numb himself to the horrors of his existence? We each have our ways of coping with our personal pain. Some are more visible than others. The recognition of our fellow man's higher self should never be used as a justification not to serve, only as a way to direct our compassion and sense of connection.

Perhaps money is not the answer in certain situations. But there's almost always something to do when we are asked for help. Jesus said that whenever we feed or clothe the poor we are in essence serving him. I can't think of a more meaningful way to honor the divine than by caring for his beloved children. Going to church or chanting, meditating, saying prayers, and lighting incense are all lovely and have their place, but the living worship of doing God's will through service is infinitely more powerful.

Charitable Contribution

So how do you extend the concept of "loving the neighbor" outward? How do you live in a way that benefits people you will never meet? The most obvious and straightforward thing is a financial donation. Most of us Americans have something to give. We are fortunate just to be living in this country—a land full of opportunity and abundance. According to the World Bank development indicators, over half the planet's population, or three billion people, live on under $2.50 per day. That's less than many of us spend on our morning latte. I encourage you to think about how greatly you've been blessed and consider sharing some of that with those in need. How much is up to you.

There's another way to contribute that I believe will enrich your life as much as it benefits those you serve—volunteering. When you actively participate in a charitable organization, you get a sense of fulfillment that writing a check can't match. (Unless, of course, it's an outrageously large check and you are single-handedly responsible for the new science wing at your alma mater.)

Neither Mehmet nor I had a ton of free time to donate, but we knew we wanted to give back to society in a way that was more than just financial. We created a foundation about a decade ago as a way of making a difference in specific areas where we were passionate. Originally Mehmet wanted to support cardiac research, thinking that given his expertise, that's where he could have the biggest impact. But after a few years it became evident that if the foundation was really going to make a dent in heart disease, we needed to address the cause rather than just looking for better ways to treat the symptoms. We realized that lifestyle was responsible for much of the disease that afflicted Mehmet's patients, and since we wanted to change people's habits, we'd better start when they were young. We initiated an educational branch of the foundation, based on the Peace Corps model, to send young college graduates into high schools to teach nutrition, physical fitness, and mental resilience to teenagers trying to stay healthy. Today, our foundation, Healthcorps, is in fifty schools across the country and reaches more than 25,000 students a year.

I know that sounds big, and it is. But when we started, we were in two New York schools with a few premed students and one administrator as volunteers. We had no idea where we were going to get money or how we would grow, but we had a vision for what we wanted to accomplish, and things began to fall into place.

If there's something that really touches you, a place where you see a need for help, do something about it. You may not have the resources to start a charity on your own, but there are tons of ways to contribute. You can raise money for your favorite foundations through organized walks, telephone campaigns, or festivals. You can wear rubber bracelets to increase awareness, gather signatures on petitions, or hand out fliers.

You can also serve directly, through houses of worship, hospitals, schools, soup kitchens, and shelters. There are lots of international opportunities too. We have several physician friends who dedicate a couple of weeks a year to working in clinics in the Third World. One family we know spends their spring breaks building homes in Central America. If you look around, you will see myriad ways to help. And once you become engaged, you will find your own life expand with new meaning and purpose.

Do What You Do

Deep down I think most of us know we're capable of making a difference and feel the need to contribute in a meaningful way, but we're easily distracted and overwhelmed by the enormity of the world's problems. Because even if you're the greatest philanthropist of all time and are well on your way to canonization, you won't be able to save everyone. And if you're just a normal person, trying to raise a family and make ends meet, you may be wondering why you should even bother.

Throwing your hands up at the immensity of global issues from poverty and disease to genocide and torture is not a conscious response. Saying it can't be solved is nothing more than an excuse to do nothing. You can pretend you're being realistic or pragmatic or that you're just too busy, but if you're honest with yourself, you'll see it's more likely laziness or fear or selfishness that's keeping you from getting involved. It's much easier to keep the blinders on and stay focused on your personal situation than to open yourself to the truth of universal human suffering. But that doesn't really benefit you or anyone else. As Fritjof Capra says, "Instead of wondering whether or not we can save the planet, it is best to ignore such trivialities and simply get to work."

So with the full knowledge that no matter what action you choose, the world will continue to be a place of pain and inequity, what can you do? Well, the first thing is to recognize that while you can't fix everything, you can fix something.

Make an honest assessment of your strengths and passions to see where your abilities are best suited. Start by asking yourself three questions: "What am I good at? What do I care deeply about? And what do I enjoy?" When you understand these things about yourself, you will begin to see your path. You have a gift. A unique

166

ability to serve in a way that no one else can. It is your privilege and your obligation to use it.

Like everything else we've talked about, deciding what type of service is right for you involves self-awareness and a commitment to a higher state of being. Yes, those are running themes in this book, but they are essential for consciously living in relationship with anyone and everyone, including those you seek to help.

It may be useful to refer back to the Enneagram when assessing your character traits as they relate to contribution. It can give you clues, not necessarily about what you should do but about how to do it. So, for example, if you're a Four and you want to volunteer as a political activist, try to bring your creative and flamboyant spirit to the experience. Don't pick something where you are kept in a boring rote activity or become just another member of a group.

Keep in mind that assisting someone else shouldn't be torture for you. For example, if you faint at the sight of blood, your call to service is probably not as an emergency medical technician. Ideally the way you choose to benefit humanity should bring you pleasure and deep satisfaction—not only because you're doing something worthwhile, but because you love doing it.

Finally, allow yourself to be led to where you may be needed most. You can call it divine providence or synchronicity or fate, but try to see what opportunities are being given to you on a daily basis. That doesn't mean that you should just sit back and wait for people in need to show up at your door. Keep your eyes open and you will see a million different paths of service to pursue. Follow one and see the possibilities unfold.

Conscious Living

I think the two biggest obstacles to a broader consciousness for modern Americans are selfishness and deliberate ignorance. I know that's a rather audacious claim and I hesitated even to write this section because I really don't want to seem preachy or to point fingers. I myself am as guilty of both these failings as anyone reading this book. But I think that they need to be examined if we are to have any chance of evolving out of our ego-based behavior.

I single out Americans not because the rest of the world is perfect, but because selfishness is a part of the very fabric of our culture. The "rugged individualism" that has in many ways made America successful has also cut us off from our collective identity. We see things as "good" when they benefit us directly and "bad" when they benefit someone other than us. We end up making every decision, whether political, economic, or social, based on how it will affect us personally. The broader societal and global ramifications of our choices are rarely considered and almost never acted upon.

Deliberate ignorance is an outgrowth of that selfishness. We want what we want and we really don't want to know what that will mean for anyone else. For example, Americans like to get stuff cheap. When we're consuming things like oil, clothing, and even food, the cost in dollars at the point of purchase is often the crucial determining factor in our decision to buy. What lies behind the low price tag can be anything from a repressive, sexist political regime to sweatshops with child labor to massive deforestation of the Amazon basin.

We don't want to hear about any of these conditions and certainly refuse to acknowledge our role in perpetuating their existence. Most worrisome of all is that we seem incapable of changing our pattern of consumption to mitigate its impact—even after the situation is brought to our attention. It's not that we don't care. We just care about getting what we want more.

I'll use the example of eating meat to illustrate because it's something I've thought about a lot. I mentioned earlier that I'm a vegetarian. I'm sure that scares a bunch of you. But let me clarify that I'm not a food fascist and I'm not trying to convince you to never eat meat again. While I personally choose not to consume flesh foods, I don't think there's anything inherently immoral in doing so. Two of my kids still eat meat and Mehmet will indulge in a side of ribs every six months or so. People have been living with animals and eating them for millennia. That's not the issue. It's how much we consume and the farming practices that gluttony necessitates that I object to.

Modern factory farms are nothing short of horrifying. The conditions are barbaric not only for the animals but for the humans working there as well (many of whom have little recourse as illegal immigrants). The rationale behind the obscenely confined spaces and unnatural feeding practices (fish and meat by-products and genetically modified corn don't sound like food for herbivores to me; what nutjob came up with that menu?) is always keeping the price of meat affordable. Yet the amount of energy that is required and wasted creating animal protein is many times more than what we would need if we were to eat lower on the food chain. And finally, there is no denying that the global consequences of this industrial farming are devastating. A 2006 United Nations report listed it as one of the top two or three threats to our environment, citing everything from air and water pollution to land degradation and loss of biodiversity. The bottom line is that mass production of meat is inhumane, inefficient, and unsustainable.

All that being said, I respect whatever choice you want to make in regard to your diet. But I urge you to choose from a place of conscious awareness, not from ignorance born of lethargy, not because you can't be bothered to think about where your food comes from. Understand the true cost of your choices.

Try to bring this thoughtfulness to other areas of consumption as well. Our mindless habits hurt our planet, our neighbors, and ourselves. No, you don't need to rush out and buy a Prius. But when you do utilize the world's bountiful resources, see if you can do so a little more sparingly. Seek to use less energy, to create less waste, and to view what you do take with gratitude rather than a sense of entitlement.

There I go, ranting like a televangelist on fire. And I said I would avoid getting all preachy. Just so we're all really clear on this, I am not going to win any conservationist of the year awards. I won't even get the Miss Congeniality prize in a philanthropy pageant. This chapter, just like every other chapter in the book, is here because it's something I struggle with myself. Attempting to live with awareness of how your behavior impacts the human collective is *hard*. It adds one more layer of complexity in an already bewildering world. (I can barely figure out if the extra calories in a piece of chocolate are worth it, let alone determine if it the cocoa beans were harvested by people earning a livable wage.)

My objective is to be present to the bigger reality, to see my own, willful desires in context of the needs of six billion other people, to avoid acting reflexively and to understand that there are ramifications to my actions. I'm not saying that *you* have to do any of this. It's your choice but one that does not affect you alone. And there's the great irony. Your personal growth is directly related to your capacity for service and vice versa. As you evolve through your own suffering, you learn to become more responsive to the suffering of all beings. And when you reach out to help others, you find that you yourself are the one healed.

Give It Up

This exercise is designed to help us shift away from seeing the world through our limited personal, tribal, or national perspective and open us to the reality of universal relationship.

DAY 1. Smile. For one day determine to smile at every single person with whom you make eye contact. It doesn't sound like much, but a smile communicates acceptance, approval, and connection. It can turn someone's day around in a microsecond. Plus you will feel great!

DAY 2. Send blessings. You can continue smiling, but today add a silent blessing of positive intention for the people you encounter. Possible thoughts include "May you be well" or "May you be free from suffering," "God grant you peace" and "Let your life be filled with grace." Find a wish for mankind that is particularly meaningful to you and spread it.

DAY 3. Use it or lose it. Go through your closets and take out everything that you haven't worn in over a year. That stack of jeans you used to fit into before the last two children should be the first to go. Cart them all down to the Salvation Army or church clothing drive and know that they will be put to much better use than cluttering your shelves. Next week you can do the same thing with the extra stuff you've got stashed in the basement, attic, or kitchen.

DAY 4. Do a one-day self-imposed tithing. For every dollar that you spend on yourself, from filling your tank up with gas to buying a fast-food lunch, put aside 10 percent. Save your receipts to tally up. Do this one day a week for the rest of the year, then give the money away. You'll be amazed at how much you've accumulated—and shocked to realize that it is only a tiny fraction of what you've personally spent.

DAY 5. Make a list of things you care passionately about but which have no direct impact on your day-to-day life. For example, Mehmet is troubled by the increasing rate of childhood obesity in this country. I get more worked up over the lack of basic human rights for women in much of the Islamic world. (Female circumcision incenses me.) But we are both deeply committed to empowering people to take charge of their own physical, emotional, and spiritual well-being. Write down at least ten things that really matter to you and notice how far your love extends.

DAY 6. Pick one area from your list and take action. Decide on a single thing that you can do to make a difference and take a step toward that goal today. It can be as simple as finding a charity that supports your cause and sending them a check for twenty dollars or writing a letter to your local congressman. You can start a petition, volunteer your time, give blood, or organize a fund-raiser. Find some way that you can change the world and do it now.

DAY 7. Start a chain reaction. Talk to your friends, family, and coworkers. See what they are profoundly moved by and inspire them to do something about it. Encourage them to get behind their convictions. If you happen to share an interest, become a team. The synergistic effect of people working together is extremely powerful.

CHAPTER 9

God

This is the part about being in relationship with God. I have to admit, it makes me a little nervous. Not God, just trying to write about God. I have very strong feelings on the subject, but it's not as if I have any evidence that what I believe is accurate. Nobody does. Even the mystics only have their personal experience—no tangible proof that God exists. So I'm not going to waste your time or mine trying to convince you of anything. Either you believe in God or you don't.

Writing about God also makes me nervous because it tends to imply that I'm a particularly virtuous person, which I'm absolutely not. I lie. I curse. You know about my proclivity for gossip. I drink. I yell. Did I mention coveting? Heck, I've broken at least half of the Ten Commandments, and that was just this morning. I don't want even for a second to give the impression that I am some goody-two-shoes, that I always obey the rules, or that I'm even all that nice. Nope, not me.

For some reason whenever people talk about God, they have to behave—or at least look like they're behaving by doing up their top button. Frankly, I don't think God gives a hoot about buttons. I think God only cares about our being in loving relationship with him and with each other. But of course I would think that. That's what this book is all about.

And though I'm neither a seer nor a saint, I'm going to try to describe what relationship with God can look like. As in each of the other chapters, I'll state things straight up, the way I see them. Feel free to disagree, object, roll your eyes. If something resonates for you, fabulous. If not, just chalk it up to the First Amendment (which covers freedom of religion as well as expression).

Just to reiterate a couple of points from the introduction (it was a long time ago), I have a habit of referring to God as "he." I was raised to see the divine as masculine and I admit I'm comfortable with that imagery for myself. But I am also quite certain that the infinite would by definition encompass every male and female attribute. I never for a moment felt that I wasn't formed in the image of God because I'm a girl. If you're more comfortable with using "she," please do so.

And again, if the term "the universe" works better for you, use that instead. Even if you're an ardent atheist, I hope that you'll find something in this chapter that speaks to you. Perhaps you can connect with a collective ethic of humanity or a sense of order within nature. Maybe like many Buddhists you can seek union with that place of inner reality or the "very subtle mind" where there is "no self." Feel free to modify anything I say so that it makes sense to you in your journey of relationship with all that is good and true and eternal. For me, a personal God is easiest to love. Attempting to generate any emotion for abstract constructs like order, beauty, or mercy is more than I'm capable of at this stage in my spiritual development. So when I speak about God, I'm going to refer to him in his divinely human form, but go ahead and insert swirling galaxies if you prefer.

A Question of Faith

Regardless of how you envision God, I believe this is your single most important relationship. According to Jung, man's fundamental desire is for union with the divine. This is what we were created for. It is the very purpose of life. Okay, some of you are thinking, "What are you talking about? I don't have a *relationship* with God." And maybe you don't, or maybe you just think you don't.

I have this sort of friend who hates God. He's angry and contemptuous and spends much of his time railing against the stupidity of human sheep who delude themselves into believing in something that's simply a product of primitive man's fearful musing. Which is cool, if his atheism is working for him. By "working" I mean, Does it inspire him to be a better person? Does it give him a reason to grow each day? Does it help him to be kinder to other people? And does it bring him joy?

I'm not saying it doesn't do all that. It may, and it's not my job to judge either way. My point in using him as an example is merely to ask this question: if he really thinks God doesn't exist, why is he wasting so much energy fighting him? Why rant and spew and blog about nothing? We don't file for divorce from imaginary people. We don't carry an umbrella if it's not raining. The irony is that in a weird way this guy's whole life is devoted to God—an entity he is convinced is a hoax. Emotionally, mentally, and energetically, he's in relationship with God. It happens to be a crappy relationship, but it's still relationship.

But we were talking about you. Let's assume if you've read this far without throwing the book across the room that you're okay with the concept of living in relationship with the divine. While many intellectual secularists would tell you that God is a social construct devised to keep order in groups, that doesn't explain the human yearning. People don't enter relationship with God because they want to be told how to behave in society, but because there's something about the human spirit that actually longs for God. And not just as an explanation for creation. We desire union with him on a very fundamental level.

Somewhere at our core we sense that we're insufficient and flawed. When we become ill or lose our job, marriage, or a loved one, we realize that all the things that *really* matter are beyond our control. We don't have the ability to face the stress of the world or even our own inner demons. That's when we have to get our strength from something outside ourselves. This is the essence of Alcoholics Anonymous—to admit that we are powerless and submit to "God, as we understand him." Connection with a higher power that really knows us and loves us anyway is the only thing that can fill the emptiness we try to escape through addiction. Nothing but reuniting with our maker ever truly satisfies.

Bound

If you had asked me fifteen years ago if I were religious, I would have responded "yes" without hesitation. Now I have to think about it a bit. I only rarely go to church and often it's a church with which I have no affiliation. I happily bring flowers to Buddhist temples, break bread at seders, and chant with Hindu gurus. There are some Sunday afternoons when I find a chapter in Dostoyevsky's *The Brothers Karamazov* more inspiring than the sermon that morning. So am I religious? I guess that depends on how you define the word.

The Latin root *religio* means "to bind fast." There are lots of ways that our modern religions attempt to bind us. Ritual, collective history, mythology, and social dictates all serve to solidify our attachment. My question here is, To what? If the purpose of an organization is to help us conjoin with God on a profound inner level, then I'm all for it. If instead its objective is to tie us more firmly to identification with a particular group, tribe, or set of opinions, excluding all others, then I'm not sure I want to be bound.

Don't get me wrong. I'm not antireligion at all. If I'm anti-anything, it's the narrow-mindedness and personal ambition of people who manipulate religion to further their own aims. And of course there's always a Bible-toting sociopathic killer, who gives anyone wearing a cross a bad name. Like anything powerful, religion can be abused by both individuals and groups to control, repress, and persecute those who threaten them. That doesn't mean the religion itself is bad. I'm always slightly annoyed by people who try to discredit Christianity by pointing to the Inquisition and the Crusades or think all of Islam is violent based on the behavior of a few radical sects. In my opinion they might as well ban sex because of rape and incest.

But I'm concerned that much of the way we practice religion today is merely increasing our ego identification rather than freeing us from it. Religion becomes a means of building false confidence and not a path of surrender and trust. Worst of all, it's used to separate us from our fellow man instead of bringing us into closer relationship.

This sort of faith tends to be based on fear—fear of the unknown, fear of "the other," and fear of who we truly are. Rather than addressing their insecurities, fearful people claim salvation and continue to act with hatred. They point to the faults of others to avoid dealing with their own. There's a cool word I just learned that describes this exactly: *antinomianism*. It means "using God's grace as an excuse to sin."

I'm not referring to a particular group here. Any doctrine can be twisted to make its followers feel superior and elect. In fact, when interpreted rigidly, most religions do claim to have exclusive access to the divine. The beauty of this language is that it makes the follower feel special. And indeed we are special. *All of us.* As we evolve we understand that God invites each one of us to special-ness. He just uses varied language and a different voice to reach different ears.

Truth is absolute, but as soon as it manifests itself in the natural realm, it passes through the filter of human capacity and is there-fore qualified. To suppose for a minute that our eight-pound brains can know the complete truth about the nature of God is ridiculous. The infinite can never be fully comprehended by the finite. As I see it, if religion is about creating a meaningful context in which we can experience God, then the ways are as many as there are individuals. Like paths up a mountain, some are long and windy, some straight and steep (deep suffering can be a pretty direct route to enlighten-ment), but if you keep heading up, you'll eventually get to the top.

I'm not a relativist. I don't think all paths are equal. Metaphori-cally, some lead directly to mineshafts while they post signs reading "Summit this way." My feeling is that if your religion makes you less loving and less compassionate, it's not serving you spiritually. True religion brings you closer to God and to your fellow man.

A Twisty Path

My own search for personal religious experience was circuitous and is ongoing. I was quite happy with the church of my childhood but felt that complacency in my spiritual life was not an option. I was motivated in part by the fact that I married a Muslim and thought that I needed to broaden my understanding of who God was for him.

During our first year of marriage I began diligently reading the Koran and after getting through about two-thirds of it determined I was ready to have an informed discussion with Mehmet on the subject. It became evident within the first five minutes that his paradigm of the universe had been shaped more by his secular education than by the teachings of his Islamic ancestry. But through our dialogue we discovered that the part of the Muslim faith we were both drawn to was Sufism, the mystical branch popularized by the thirteenth-century poet Rumi which focuses primarily on falling in love with the divine. This idea of God as the "beloved" was a new concept for me. I'd always thought I "loved" God, but it was definitely from a respectful distance. It was sort of like the relationship I had with my high school principal. I admired her, I had affection for her, and I was a little bit afraid of her. This was not the sort of adoration Rumi spoke of.

Rapturous devotion is not a common state for me, and I confess I was a bit fearful of what passionate spirituality might look like. I didn't want the route of intense suffering that many of the Christian mystics had experienced. Nor was I drawn to long bouts of sitting in deep meditation and disengaging from the world. But I was curious and wanted to find some way to connect with God on an emotional level.

I decided to delve deeper into Christianity, so I enrolled in classes at Union Theological Seminary. I dropped out after a year. It wasn't what I was looking for. I had no interest in the Bible as a work of literature or its sociohistoric context. Nor did I think a working knowledge of Hebrew or Greek would deepen my connection to the divine. I didn't want a theoretical knowledge about God. What I longed for was a deeper relationship with him.

Since I had been frustrated by the more orthodox approach, I turned to the New Age authors. I read everyone from Carlos Castaneda, Caroline Myss, and Marianne Williamson to Deepak Chopra, Joan Borysenko, Ram Dass, and Eckhart Tolle. I picked up anything in the self-help and spirituality sections. There was a lot of great stuff, but I found that for the most part the New Age movement wasn't really my thing.

Yeah, I know. I sound like a spiritual Goldilocks. "This one's too hot. This one's too cold." But what I discovered while I was stomping around like a little malcontent was that the porridge pot itself was "just right."

I noticed that when any teaching clicked for me, it was always in those places of overlap with some ancient tradition. I had studied Buddhism in college and had read parts of the Rig Veda and the Bhagavad Gita in a comparative religion class at Union. There was (and is) tremendous collective spiritual wisdom all over the world. I began searching through books on Kabbalah and medieval alchemy and fell in love with classical mythology, especially as explained by Joseph Campbell.

What intrigued me most were the places where they all converged. There is some variant of the Ten Commandments in just about every faith. No religion thinks it's okay to murder, or steal, or commit adultery. You could say that this is just because these are laws that an agrarian society would need in place to ensure stability. But I think it's more. Stories of a great flood and references to a tree of life are found universally. I was instantly drawn to the similarities among texts, but I also grew to appreciate the differences, as each one expressed another aspect of the infinite divine.

The more I saw the "many faces of God" reflected in the world, the more I saw him directly in my own life. The story of humanity's search for meaning through struggle and union with the divine—the rejection, the stumbling, the ecstasy, the embrace—this was my story too. We all look for God (go ahead and insert "purpose" or "significance" if you must), turn away, falter, doubt, trust, reject, and love. This is the nature of man's glorious dance with God. This is relationship.

My Religion

My particular and personal view of God is one based on the writings of Emanuel Swedenborg. Since so much of how I think about life and relationship is colored by his doctrine, I thought it would be useful to explain it. Please don't interpret this as an attempt to convert you. What you believe is your business, not mine. My hope for you is that you have a conviction—religious or otherwise—that provides you with meaning and connection. That's what my faith does for me.

So let me start with a very brief overview of some of what I was taught about God—or at least what I learned about God (because sometimes what is heard is different from what is said). For those of you who coincidentally happen to be Swedenborg scholars, I'm not going for the definitive treatise on Swedenborgian theology here. I've left out stuff and broadly interpreted the rest. This is just what I tell my friends when they ask me about my religion.

First off, we believe that God's essence is love and wisdom. He is the source of all good and all truth, and evil is the result of mankind's choice to turn away from that love and indulge selfish, materialistic desires instead. Humans must be able to choose evil in order to remain in spiritual freedom. If we are compelled to choose good, it is no choice at all.

God loves saints and sinners alike. We're all both on any given day. As fallible humans we can never earn God's love through adherence to any moral code. By our very nature we are imperfect and prone to make mistakes. But God is absolute mercy, always seeking to draw us to himself. Often it is through our times of failure that he is best able to effect union with us. Those places where our ego cracks are a way for him to enter our lives once we reject our selfish loves and turn to him.

God condemns no one. It's our own withdrawal that makes us feel judged. Just as we can hide ourselves in a cave to escape the sun's rays, we can emotionally block the perception of God's love flowing into our lives. But our choosing the dark doesn't mean the sun's not shining. And shutting our hearts to divine presence is our issue, not God's. We sometimes feel that God's punishing us when we sin, but it's actually the sin itself that causes us to suffer. When we decide to reject a behavior because it's harmful to ourselves and others and choose instead a life of compassion, we can see that God has been there all along.

There is one God with three aspects—the Father, Son, and Holy Spirit. In Swedenborgian doctrine, the Trinity is seen as a separation not of persons but of divine qualities. Just as humans have a soul, a body, and a mind, so the one God has an interior, a physical manifestation, and activity in the created universe. In this light, Jesus isn't a separate being but the incarnation of the divine itself.

Swedenborgians also deny the traditional notion of atonement. We don't perceive Jesus as a sacrificial offering to appease an angry Jehovah. His gift of salvation was and is to provide a means for us to approach him directly and to show us a living example of the path of spiritual rebirth or regeneration.

One of Swedenborg's key teachings is that the Bible is the word of God and as such is divine truth itself, though it may not seem like it at first glance. If you read through the Bible, you can't help but notice that it's full of inconsistencies and contradictions. For example, God is portrayed as both benevolent and wrathful, and in the creation story plants are produced a full day before the sun and moon appear on the scene. Taken as a moral guide, the Bible tends to be fairly confusing. Abraham pretends his wife, Sarah, is just his sister and allows her to be taken into a foreign king's harem. Jacob steals his brother's blessing by tricking his blind father, and David murders one of his generals because he lusts for the man's wife. There aren't a whole lot of truly virtuous people to be found.

We're taught that what makes the Bible divine is its internal sense and that the truth of the Bible is clothed in appearance and parable. Each story is written in what Swedenborg calls the language of correspondences, which is a representative interface between the material and spiritual realms. The Bible, then, is not merely a historical account of the children of Israel but a detailed description of the spiritual journey each one of us takes as we regenerate from purely natural to spiritual beings.

The idea of an inner meaning within the Bible is not exclusive to Swedenborg. In fact, this teaching is the basis of the Zohar, the primary book of kabbalistic wisdom, as well. And the whole field of hermeneutics, or biblical interpretation, implies by its very existence that even Christians see layered and nuanced meaning within the literal sense.

Some people argue that by interpreting the Bible metaphorically, we lose its authority. I think the opposite is true. Assuming the Bible is to be taken in only a literal way actually makes *us*, the reader, have to determine what is divinely ordained. We end up needing to decide what is relevant and applicable—what we will or won't adhere to. There's not a single fundamentalist who follows the Bible *exactly*. No one sacrifices young bullocks or turtledoves anymore or stones their children for behaving badly. And it's not just the Old Testament that we fudge. When was the last time you met someone who "plucked out" his eye because it "offended" him? Certainly when Jesus spoke about putting our "light under a bushel," he was speaking symbolically. But who decides when Jesus meant what he *said* or when he meant something else?

I once had a disagreement with a very well known evangelical minister who assured me that everyone who had not professed faith in Jesus was going to hell. He claimed that Jesus' statement "I am the way, the truth and the life; no one cometh to the Father but by me" was evidence of this fact.

I explained to him that Swedenborgians believe that what Christ was referring to was his *essence*, not his physical body. Attaining salvation "through" him means living according to the path he taught, which is one of compassion and service toward others. This, anyone of any faith can achieve, hence heaven is accessible to all. He told me I was wrong. I muttered something about there being several billion reasons I hoped I wasn't and excused myself.

Which brings us to the concept of heaven and hell. Swedenborg says that these are not places but states. Heaven is made up of people who share a common love for God and the neighbor, and hell is home to those who prefer the world and themselves. Living in one or the other is neither a punishment nor a reward but a reflection of who we are as an expression of what we love. He also explains that we are there right now.

According to Swedenborg we exist on both the physical and spiritual planes simultaneously. Even now, when we indulge our evil inclinations, our spirits are in a hellish state and are subject to hellish influence. When we act from compassion and truth, we open ourselves to heavenly influx. After death, we continue in the state we have chosen while on earth. We live on as either angels or evil spirits based on where our affections lie. In effect we become what we love.

Talking with God

One of the essentials in any relationship is communication. We converse with God using song and silence, celebration and lamentation. But mostly our dialogue with the divine is through prayer.

I grew up saying the Lord's Prayer every night and still say it with my children when I put them to bed. There are many evenings when I recite the words by rote, but when I pay attention, I realize how beautiful this prayer actually is.

It starts with "Our Father," which is an appreciation of our identity as God's children, and also of the collective nature of humanity. We do not pray "My Father." This opening address describes both our relationship with God and our relationship to each other.

We then recognize the sacred nature of our invocation with the reverential "hallowed be thy name," maintaining an attitude of humility as we approach the divine. We open ourselves to God by inviting his "Kingdom" into our lives and agree to the subjugation of our selfish desires by submitting to his will.

By asking for our "daily bread" we recognize that all good things are from him and commit to living in the present moment. (Note, it is not "this week's bread" or "bread for the rest of our lives.")

We ask to be forgiven and acknowledge that it is our own forgiveness of others that opens us to God's love. We see that holding on to bitterness and anger prevents us from fully experiencing the joy that comes from receiving true mercy and grace.

In the next line we pray to avoid temptation and evil, asserting that all good is from him and confessing that we are powerless against hellish impulses without his aid. And we close with exclamations of praise, reconfirming our trust in God's omnipotence.

I love this prayer and think if it's said with full intention in a state of humble gratitude, this short supplication can fill all your spiritual dialoguing needs. But it doesn't have to be exclusive. Heck, you don't have to use it at all—especially if you're not Christian. As I mentioned, I say it with my kids before bed, but these days my own prayer tends to be more informal and sporadic. Sometimes it's quick and to the point, like a text message: "Hey God, thanks for helping me get through that phone call without incident." On other occasions it turns into long, drawn-out ramblings in which I attempt to make sense of my life. Often it's just quiet time, when I try to remain open to the presence of the divine.

This inner silence has been a really valuable tool in shifting how I talk with God. For one thing it's helped me be aware of how much I seek to control him. I know that sounds a little crazy. How could I, a mere mortal, try to control the omnipotent creator of the universe? Hmm, let's see . . . The methods I've used include begging, bargaining, bribing ("If you just let me get through this, I promise I will never ever use your name in vain."), rationalizing, threatening ("How can I believe in you if . . ."), coaxing, cajoling, sulking, and crying. Sound familiar?

We end up using prayer as an opportunity to make requests, register complaints, and express our general frustration over the fact that God's not running things the way we'd like. It's not that we can't talk to him about those things. God listens no matter what the topic of conversation, but keeping it at that level is not transformative.

We need (and I am a big part of that "we") to learn to have faith in divine providence. This involves developing an attitude of appreciation for what is, even when it's not what we want. Once we trust that God knows what he's doing, our prayers become more of an intimate sharing than a shopping list. We see that the real purpose of prayer is to change our hearts, not to change God's mind. (What kind of God would actually be swayed by the forty-seventh time we asked for a raise—but not the forty-sixth?) The goal of cultivating faith is to finally give up thinking we know what's best and let our solitary prayer be "Thy will be done."

You and God

What does being in relationship with God look like? For some it's ecstatic; others find it a deep source of comfort through periods of intense suffering. For me, it's an ongoing dialogue in my head, which is both verbal and directly intuitive. I derive a real sense of connection from the conversation, but I can never be absolutely sure I'm not just talking to myself.

For you, I'm sure the relationship is entirely different. Maybe God's companionship is something you experience only once in a while. It could be as subtle as seeing a glimmer of divinity in your child's smile or hearing God's whisper in the gentle song of the mourning dove. Or it may be as overt as having a date night with God by watching a particularly charismatic minister on television. Whatever your experience ends up looking like, know that it is intensely personal and absolutely unique. You and God are one of a kind.

In many ways your relationship with God is similar to your relationships with people. Ideally they're all built on intimacy, trust, understanding, and love. One thing to remember is that you are a crucial part of the team. God loves you no matter what, but for you to experience that love fully, you need to participate. Do you invite God into your life? If so, is it only when you want something you can't get for yourself? Also, what do you bring to the table? Are you honest, receptive, and generous in the relationship? Are you committed to union?

Relationships grow through the participants' spending time together. How do you spend time with God? Well, there are several ways. The first is just to be open to his presence. Notice the divine order in nature—in everything from the design of a leaf to the cycle of the seasons. Sunsets are an exquisite reminder of the splendor and majesty of the Lord, but the seemingly commonplace occurrence of dew or the sprouting of dandelions through a concrete sidewalk is equally miraculous.

Look for the specialness of everyday events. Sadly, we have become inured to the truly amazing quality of all that surrounds us. Things as routine as putting on lipstick or walking your child to the school bus take on new meaning when you examine them at a deeper level. Every moment has significance if you open your eyes. And I don't just mean for you personally, as part of the synchronistic wonder of your life. There's a universal story in each event.

Take the lipstick example. It doesn't seem like a particularly profound activity, but when you see it as part of a deeply ingrained desire to attract the opposite sex by mimicking a sign of fertility, it becomes more interesting. Explore the idea further and you'll see that the expression of female sexuality has been highly taboo for millennia and is still forbidden in many parts of the world. (Ironically, the mother and the whore both obtain their identity through the same act.) The suppression of women as sexual beings was in part to ensure fidelity, thereby protecting inheritance of property within families, but it also encompasses something more—something deep and archetypal about the feminine ideal as receptive and yielding rather than aggressive and active. The whole debate, struggle, historical context, and current position are expressed through the lipstick when you look beneath the surface.

Learning to think this way was one of the acting exercises taught by Ivan (my teacher from chapter 2). It was called "looking for the extraordinary in the ordinary." He would give us a simple scene—say, a cat on a windowsill. Then he would ask us to be very specific about the details. Is the cat a purebred or a stray? Well fed or neglected? Is it asleep or grooming or hunting insects? We would make the image as precise as possible. Once we had that down, we had to go deep. What was the cat's relationship with the humans in its life? How was this reflective of the archetypal bond between man and beast? What role has the domestication of the cat played in the history of mankind? How has it contributed to the very development of civilization?

When you develop the ability to use this sort of X-ray vision, you begin to see that no single image is as simple as it seems. Nothing is meaningless. Every moment is significant. The sacred lives within the mundane.

Spend time in meditation or contemplation. Relationship involves dialogue, not monologue, so you need to quiet your own voice if you want to sense God with you. There are many different methods of stilling your mind. I've used centering prayer, yogic breathing techniques, walking meditations, guided imagery, and transcendental meditation. The aim in each one is to become fully aware of the present moment, but different methods are better suited to different personality types. You need to pick one that is both pleasant (so you do it regularly) and effective.

If you're completely new to meditation, I suggest starting with a simple breath observation. Sit comfortably and close your eyes. Bring your attention to the act of inhaling and exhaling. To stay focused, you can actively notice any sensation the breathing generates, from your nose to your throat and down into your chest. If thoughts come up (and they will), don't chastise yourself or try to force them out. Simply notice them and allow them to drift away by gently bringing your awareness back to your breath.

As you develop your own meditative process, you'll find yourself becoming more centered and peaceful. In this state, allow yourself to be receptive to God's influx. It may seem like nothing more than a shift in your perception, or it could be clouds of glory. However you experience the numinous, it will probably not be what you expect.

Play an active role in your spiritual education. It's easy to become complacent and intellectually lazy. Don't take everything your minister, priest, rabbi, or imam says at face value. Go to the source yourself. Read the sacred texts of your tradition. See what they really say. Look for where they speak to you directly. Let them stimulate you to think, to question, to rejoice, and to love.

Broaden your understanding of how God has revealed him/herself in the world by going to a religious service of a faith other than the one you were born into. Read their literature, sing their songs, see a dimension of God that you never imagined. Look specifically for places of overlap and similarity. Embrace the variety of forms of universal truth and try to remain open to ideas that could expand or enrich your connection with the singular divinity behind the manifest diversity.

Finally, pray. Allow your prayer to come from your innermost being, unencumbered by selfish desire. Let it be a prayer of gratitude and praise, surrender and trust. Ask that you may become a vessel of divine light and your relationships a means of spreading that light in the world.

EXERCISE

New Religion

DAY 1. Start keeping a spiritual journal. This is something like a diary, but rather than writing about the physical things that happen during the day, record your inner life. You can keep track of feelings, insights, and observations. You may want to jot down ways you noticed yourself reacting as your typical Enneagram number or moments when you were able to resist the urge to behave selfishly. Express your struggles and your fears but don't forget to celebrate your internal triumphs.

DAY 2. Draw a picture of how you see God. Don't be inhibited by a perceived lack of artistic abilities. Your image can be totally abstract or as straightforward as a bearded old man on a throne. Just try to express some of the qualities that your vision of God embodies. Next, draw a picture of yourself. Here again, the same principles apply. This exercise is about seeing who you are, not how well you draw. When you're done, examine the two pages and notice the qualities in you that are a reflection of the divine—a miracle "in the image and likeness of God."

DAY 3. Chart your life up until now and look for God in the events. Circle the times you were at your lowest and found the strength to get through. Also mark the high points in your life and notice how you were led there by a specific sequence of seeming coincidences. Look for all the places of synchronicity or guidance that may not have been visible at the time but in retrospect become very clear.

DAY 4. Create a meaningful ritual for yourself. Make it simple enough that you can do it every day but different from your regular routine. Give the action a specific meaning. For example, you can place a candle at the table before the evening meal, invoking the sacred nature of eating. As you light it, say a silent prayer that the food you are about to eat will be utilized in bringing your light into the world.

DAY 5. Write your own creed. This is a personal declaration of faith. You can use elements from your historic religion, but try to pick things that resonate strongly for you. Avoid stating things in the negative, so for example, if you don't believe in a personal God, rather than stating that directly, you could instead say, "I believe in the inherent goodness of humanity and a complex order to the universe."

DAY 6. Take a problem you haven't been able to solve and bring it to God. Start by closing your eyes and taking several deep, cleansing breaths. When you're emotionally calm, hand over your problem by admitting that it's too big for you to handle on your own. Allow your mind to settle into quiet again. Continue the deep breathing and try to let go of all thought. Once you're back to a centered place, ask God to use this problem for your greatest spiritual good. That may be taking the problem away, or it may be giving you the strength to live with it. Trust that God will help you and briefly express your gratitude. Clear your mind of all thought one more time. Then remain seated in silence until you feel ready to open your eyes and reengage your day with a sense of equanimity.

DAY 7. Engage in silent prayer. For several minutes allow yourself to dwell in the presence of the divine, asking for nothing, seeking nothing, saying nothing. Try to just exist in union.

CHAPTER 10

Integration

By now I'm pretty sure you've gotten the message that relationships are important. Goodness knows I've said it every way I can imagine. Of course there are bound to be some of you who still think the whole thing's nonsense, who believe that you are perfectly self-sufficient and independent—a veritable incarnation of Nietzsche's *übermensch*.

But I'd bet most of you probably sense that your relationships are an integral part of your existence. In many ways they determine who you are. Just as a note becomes music through its combination with other notes and a point in space is defined relative to other points, so we manifest ourselves through our interactions with those around us.

Being social creatures, we yearn for connection, for that recognition that we are part of something bigger. But there is also resistance—a feeling that just as a drop of rain disappears when it falls into the ocean, so we too lose our identity when we merge into the great collective. These conflicting urges create the dynamic dance of union and separation that we all engage in over the course of our lives.

I can't tell you how to get around this inconsistency of desire for simultaneous community and autonomy. As with all the great mysteries of life, it is more important to experience it than to understand it. As humans we love each other and we hate each other, but the bottom line is we *need* each other. We need each other to grow, to create, to evolve. Living in relationship enables us to break free of our ego-centered bonds and transcend our inauthentic self. When we live in love—with ourselves, with our fellow man, and with God—we see that we are actually much more than we ever dreamed. We are not just a drop in the ocean, we *are* the ocean.

No Static

I recently visited a beautiful little church in a New Jersey beach town. At the beginning of the sermon the minister, Sharline Fulton, said, "Only God is. We are always becoming." Initially I thought it was one of those cute phrases that look good in bathroom books or on bumper stickers and wrote it off as irrelevant. But for some reason the words kept popping back into my head through the entire service, and as I fumbled along to an unfamiliar hymn, it finally hit me that the adage provided an important key in understanding the nature of relationship.

As material entities, we are delineated by time. God, being outside the confines of space or time, can exist infinitely everywhere and always. We however, cannot. Who we are now is not who we were yesterday or who we will be tomorrow. We are always changing, whether by choice or circumstance, from one moment to the next, thus living in a perpetual state of becoming.

It's because we're not the same person over time that our relationships are more of a work in progress than a fixed entity. They are always in flux—shifting from one state to another depending on where we are at a specific point in time. There is no such thing as "happily ever after." This is the great myth that fairy tales perpetuate. Relationships don't reach a level and stay there indefinitely. We don't get married and live out the rest of our days in unmitigated bliss. Nor do we defeat the enemy (whether internal or external) and ensure everlasting peace. Our relationships can only be defined in the now—as what they are in this precise moment. In a year, a week, even an hour, we will be different, so our relationships will be different.

This motile quality of relationships means that we need to stay engaged. We can never allow ourselves to be complacent because a relationship seems good. Just like living creatures, relationships need to be cared for and nourished, otherwise they wither and die. Also, we shouldn't become despondent if our relationships are not as intimate or productive as we would like. We can improve them at any time by bringing conscious presence to each encounter.

Relationships either move toward greater intimacy, trust, and affection or shift away from those states. But the direction is almost never linear. We go up and down, get closer, then become more distant, are briefly elated, then fall into despair. The objective is to move toward integration and improvement so that while there are fluctuations, the general trend is upward.

Takeaways

So here we are, at the end of our journey together. It's time for you to click your ruby slippers and get back to Kansas—metaphorically speaking. But before you go, I have a few parting words. The Wizard, aka Mehmet, told me I needed to write you a brief summary of the key points from the previous chapters. I have to say I was reluctant. The thing about relationships is that there are no Cliffs-Notes—no easy manual of techniques you can memorize. There's no one way or even million ways to do relationships right. Relationships are about process rather than results. Frequently the lesson is the experience itself. It can't easily be reduced to a catalogue of how-tos.

But just in case you're the type of person who doesn't do well with long-form, here are the takeaway lessons for me—the equivalent of the diploma, the heart-shaped clock, and the medal of courage. These insights won't create deeper, more satisfying relationships for you, but they may help you to do it yourself.

Take inventory. Right now see if your relationships are where you want them to be. Some may be great, others may be in the toilet—which is only a real problem if you're unaware of it. You can't grow if you don't acknowledge where you are. So examine each of your primary relationships and make an honest assessment of their quality at this moment.

"They're okay" is not an acceptable answer. What that really means is "They're not good but I'm not willing to work on them." This lack of commitment to the most significant areas of your life both leads to and is a result of the addictive behavior most of us engage in. We feel empty, unfilled, without real purpose or passion. We don't like the feeling, so we eat, watch TV, shop, talk on the phone, take antidepressants, or browse the Internet to numb the gnawing anxiety that haunts each day. Though these activities mask the pain, they also prevent us from actually making the effort to lead a joy-filled, connected, meaningful life.

When looking at your relationships, make sure to consider each of the three levels: first with yourself, then with those around you, and finally with a higher power. Remember that they are inter-related and that one area out of balance will directly impact the other two. But also know that working on any of them will improve them all.

Be honest, first with yourself and then with the people in your life. Remember there are lots of ways to lie. Justification, excuses, and exaggeration are just a few of the methods we use to avoid the fact that what we're doing isn't working.

Lying is the biggest threat to real growth and personal development, and we all do it all the time. For some of us self-deception makes our choices bearable, but it never actually makes them better. To uncover the ways in which *you* are less than truthful, make a list with three categories: 1. lies you tell yourself, 2. lies you tell other people, 3. lies you tell God. It may take a while. Don't just give up if nothing comes to you right away. It could be days or even weeks before you become comfortable enough to reveal—even to yourself—the extent of your dishonesty.

Once you have a list of at least ten items, choose just one to work on for the next month. (You can tackle another one next month.) When I did this, I picked the "she said, then *I* said" embellishment. Often when telling a story about a previous conversation, especially one that is somewhat confrontational, I have a habit of recounting it with a few poetic flourishes. They usually begin with "and I was, like . . . ," which pretty much means "I thought but didn't actually say" but gives the impression that I was much tougher in the argument. I'll also conveniently forget any portion of the dialogue that portrays the other person in a favorable light. Just noticing my attempt to color the facts in this sort of situation increases my awareness of other areas where I subtly try to stretch the truth.

Observe yourself. We talked about this in chapter 1, but it warrants repeating. If you take nothing else from this book, learn to separate the personality-driven, ego-based projection of who you are from your true self. Using the Enneagram to identify the way you respond to fear can be useful, but it's not imperative. What is necessary is the ability to emotionally disengage from your habitual attachments. The best way I've found is just to be a nonjudgmental witness in all your relationships. Whether it's while you're thinking about your own needs, responding to a lover, or praying to your creator, allow part of yourself to step back and ask a few key questions. What am I feeling? What's really going on here? What do I actually want? Once you start to separate from your false self, you can engage in your relationships by responding consciously rather than reacting reflexively.

Be there. Sleepwalking through life isn't an option if you want satisfying relationships. Whether you're confronting your own emotions or dealing with a friend, you can't do it on autopilot. Our inability to be fully present is a big part of why our relationships fail and we feel disconnected and isolated. To make our interactions genuine and satisfying at the deepest level, we need to be where we are, not somewhere else.

When I feel my attention drifting or my mind wandering, there are a couple of tricks I use to bring myself back to what's going on around me. The first isn't much of a trick, it's just forcing myself to listen to what's being said. For example, my son, Oliver, likes to tell me about his inventions. Often it will be while I'm in the middle of making dinner, so I'll just nod and say, "Oh, that's nice," which is unsatisfying for him and just boring for me. If I stop chopping veggies and actually pay attention to him—make eye contact, examine the diagram, and respond with real interest—then he feels that I care about him, I gain some insight into the workings of my child's mind, and we both feel closer.

It's important to listen not just to the words but to the subtext. Pay attention to the intention behind the conversation. Also, be aware of what your motivations are. What do you want to communicate and is it coming across?

Another thing I do to stay in the moment is to heighten awareness of my environment on a sensory level. I'll try to discern ambient sounds and smells, temperature and texture. I look closely at the space I'm in and the faces of those with me. This practice always brings my focus back to where I am rather than some imagined other place or time.

Let go of the need to control others and learn to change yourself instead. For me this is the most difficult of the suggestions. I'm uncomfortable with the idea of letting other people (particularly those close to me) live in a way that is even semiautonomous. But as I mentioned in chapter 5, you can't force anyone to be anything other than who they are. The best way to change a situation is to change yourself. Do that, and you change everything. (When I finally master it, I'll let you know.)

Live large. Whatever you choose to do, do it fully and do it well. Push yourself beyond your perceived limits. Don't squander your potential because of fear; that only leads to resentment and regret. Take risks, seize opportunities, follow your dreams.

Be kind. It sounds so simple and self-evident that you may wonder why I would even mention it. The reason? Take a look around you and notice how people speak to their children, their spouses, even total strangers. We can barely be civil, let alone kind. We know how we're supposed to treat people, but doing so is another story. So I feel the need to remind you (and myself) one more time: let the Golden Rule be your guide.

Okay, that's pretty much all I know about relationships. I'll let you get back to your life and the wonderful, challenging, unique interactions that shape you and give your experience meaning. It's there in the day-to-day that everything we talked about takes form and becomes real. So go home to Uncle Henry and Auntie Em, your kids and coworkers, spouse and neighbors. I hope our time together will help you see them with new eyes—to embrace them and cherish them and know that your relationships are your true home.

Exercise

With this chapter you have a single exercise. Get this one down and you can forget about all the others.

DAY 1. *Love.* That's it. Love God. Love yourself. Love the world and everyone in it. Love passionately. Hold nothing back. Open your heart and allow yourself to be vulnerable, even when it feels dangerous. Let all your relationships be based on love and you'll be just fine. In the words of my favorite band, "Love. Love. Love . . . All you need is love."

Do this for the next seven days. Do it for the rest of your life.

Acknowledgments

Writing this book was a total pain in the butt. Honestly, I am not one of those people who can just sit down and have the pages flow from their fingertips. I perseverate over each letter. I surf the Internet. I call my friends. I make tea. Boy, do I make tea. Pots and pots have been sacrificed in the name of *US*.

Left to my own devices, I would still be rearranging the outline and procrastinating. Mercifully, there are amazing people in my life who have coaxed, prodded, and threatened me into a state of semi-productivity. The fact that I have anything on paper is due entirely to them. I love all of them and am permanently in their debt.

First and foremost among those soon to be sainted is my obscenely patient writing coach, Victoria Rowan. I would have fired me ten times over and this woman never flinched. All right, she did flinch occasionally. But then she put up her dukes and laughingly guided me back to the task at hand. She met all my attempts to avoid real work with a smile and a constant reminder to embrace my identity as a writer.

My sister Emily was invaluable as an editor, companion, and kindred spirit. I think she's the one person who knows *exactly* what I'm talking about on these pages and in life in general. I also want to thank her husband, Scott Smith, whose editing skills were spot-on and deeply appreciated.

ACKNOWLEDGMENTS

Equally crucial to this endeavor is my mother, Emily Jane Lemole. She is the only individual I know who actually lives the ideals I talk about in the book. Her partnership with my father has been the foundation and inspiration for everything I do.

Samantha and George Griffith both contributed creatively and George saved my a** by backing up my manuscript when I was having issues with my computer.

There are no stories about my other siblings, Laura and Ben Du Pont, Michael and Ruth Lemole, and Christopher and Sonia Lemole, because frankly there was no drama worthy of repetition. As a family they have been a delight, and I want to thank them for that.

My agent, Jennifer Rudolph Walsh—so smart and insightful, and utterly ferocious when it comes to business—was confident and passionate about this book when it was merely embryonic.

The team at Free Press is the best! I am so grateful to Carolyn Reidy, Carisa Hays, Suzanne Donahue, Jill Siegel, Nancy Inglis, Jennifer Weidman, Laura Cooke, Megan Clancy, and Eric Fuentecilla. I also need to give an extra special thank-you to my wonderful editor, Dominick Anfuso, his super bright and sweet assistant editor, Leah Miller, and my incomparable publisher, Martha Levin, who were unbelievably supportive and trusting. There were days when I was tempted to pick up the phone and tell them I was returning their advance, but the thought of disappointing them always got me back to the computer. You are all a huge part of this book.

Michelle Bouchard—stalwart and steadfast, a friend for life. She was one of the extremely few people with whom I felt safe enough to share the early chapters. Her encouragement kept me writing through the toughest periods.

Sue Novick, my favorite dining companion and dear friend. She was the sounding board for every story in here. There were entire lunches where she barely uttered a word as I rambled on about my latest relationship adventure. Never once did she say "enough about you, already." Nor did she make me feel guilty for the countless lunches I missed because of my evil procrastinating ways.

Christy Mack is my favorite mentor. Her grace, compassion, and generosity in all of her relationships are awe-inspiring.

Jennifer Ashton, a stellar example of personal achievement (this woman gives Mehmet a run for his money), provided a beautiful, distraction-free workspace when I finally decided to get serious.

Kathy Freston has been so helpful on so many levels. I love her passion and commitment and am deeply honored to call her my friend.

Dean Ornish was the fix-it guy who got me through some of my toughest slumps. I am so touched by his genuine warmth and caring.

Mike Roizen has been an absolute dream to work with on the YOU books for the past six years. He is truly one of the sweetest and sharpest people I know.

I'd also like to thank:

My former minister, fellow seeker, and researcher, Robert Mcclusky.

My gifted teachers Prescott Rogers, Ivan Kronenfeld, and Allen Savage. Intellectual rock stars that bunch.

My spiritual icons/gurus, Richard Rohr and Peter Rhodes. They possess wisdom beyond words.

My cheerleaders and coaches, Martha Beck and Cheryl Richardson. I am so immensely privileged to have you two on my team.

Other people who were important to this effort include: Sifu Karl Romain, my kung fu master who taught me much more than martial arts. Joel Harper, who has tried nineteen different ways to get me into shape. Diane Amato, Donna O'Sullivan, and Eileen Mckeirnan, for kindly managing my life while I checked out. And Aleida Valcarcel, Necmiye and Turgut Kacaroglu, Mike Wujek, and Nixon for holding down the home front.

ACKNOWLEDGMENTS

Finally I need to thank my children, Daphne, Arabella, Zoe, and Oliver, who helped me really understand what I was writing by *not* being patient or understanding, constantly reminding me that "living in relationship" is about being with the people around you, not buried in the hypothetical pages of an emerging book. They are amazing and I adore them.

And mostly I want to thank my true love, Mehmet. I would not be me without you.